BOYCOTTS AND DIXIE CHICKS

BOYCOTTS AND DIXIE CHICKS

CREATIVE POLITICAL PARTICIPATION AT HOME AND ABROAD

BY

ANDREW S. MCFARLAND

Paradigm Publishers
Boulder • London

Copyright © 2011 Paradigm Publishers

Published in the United States by Paradigm Publishers, 2845 Wilderness Place, Suite 200, Boulder, CO 80301 USA.

Paradigm Publishers is the trade name of Birkenkamp & Company, LLC, Dean Birkenkamp, President and Publisher.

Library of Congress Cataloging-in-Publication Data

McFarland, Andrew S., 1940–
  Boycotts and Dixie Chicks : creative political participation at home and abroad / by Andrew S. McFarland.
     p. cm.
  Includes bibliographical references and index.
  ISBN 978-1-59451-819-5 (hardcover : alk. paper)
  ISBN 978-1-59451-820-1 (pbk. : alk. paper)
  1. Political participation. I. Title.
  JF799.M34 2010
  323'.042—dc22

                                                              2010000841

Printed and bound in the United States of America on acid-free paper that meets the standards of the American National Standard for Permanence of Paper for Printed Library Materials.

Designed and Typeset by Straight Creek Bookmakers.

15 14 13 12 11   1 2 3 4 5

Dedicated to my niece, Heather Haddon

CONTENTS

Introduction

My concern for creative political participation grows out of my previous concern for the study of public-interest lobbying in Washington, D.C. From 1968 to 1975 especially, new environmental and political reform lobbies appeared in the nation's capital to an almost startling degree. This was apparently an important new political phenomenon, which Jeffrey Berry and I were among the first to study. From 1974 to 1985, I spent about half my time in Washington, learning about the policy process, interviewing public-interest-group participants, and having discussions with other scholars with similar goals in Washington. Subsequently, I published three volumes about public-interest groups: *Public Interest Lobbies: Decision Making on Energy* (1976), *Common Cause: Lobbying in the Public Interest* (1984), and *Cooperative Pluralism: The National Coal Policy Experiment* (1993), the latter about negotiations among environmentalists and coal-industry executives.

While I strove to maintain academic objectivity, I did conclude that public-interest lobbies play an important role in the American constitutional order as a means to represent the widely diffused interests in a clean environment and in the elimination of corrupt government practices. Many political scientists and lawyers might prefer to rely on the law and the state to control pollution and political corruption, but I believe that political pressure must bolster legal practice to balance the power of economic-producer interests within a capitalist system. However, while writing these three books, I concluded that environmental lobbies and Common Cause will have continuing and substantial influence, and so my concerns shifted to the identification and prescription of other means to represent dispersed public interests. (I, of course, with enthusiasm support student participation in presidential and legislative election campaigns.)

Public-interest lobbies are a vital supplement to voting, campaigning, and the mechanisms of civic engagement. The concern for civic engagement has recently been a dominant research and intellectual trend in political science, following Robert Putnam's brilliant book *Bowling Alone: The Collapse and Revival of American Community* (2000). Civic engagement focuses on continuing face-to-face interaction among people who thereby learn to trust one another and to build "social capital" as a basis for enhancing cooperation for joint action. Robert Putnam and Theda Skocpol, among others, have found a decline in civic engagement in America since the 1950s. Unfortunately for the reputation of public-interest lobbies, both Putnam and Skocpol find that they are not based on civic engagement but constitute part of the decline in American community in that they consist of elite managers and lobbyists located in Washington, dependent upon checkbook contributors, most of whom never meet in a face-to-face manner. My research is cited as one basis for such observations.

I reacted to the Putnam and Skocpol allegations of public-interest elitism with the belief that while a major contribution to democratic theory, civic-engagement theory does not state everything we need to know about democratic political participation. In particular, I concluded that political participation is a concept similar in structure to political representation, as analyzed by Hanna Fenichel Pitkin in her landmark book *The Concept of Representation* (1967). Pitkin argued that there are separable concepts of representation and that political scientists should be aware of how they use the different types of representation and the functions of each. For instance, a subordinate may represent his boss (one type); a governing committee may be concerned with descriptive representation, that is, the committee membership being proportional to group membership in terms of categories such as sex or race (a second type); King George I of England (1714 to 1727) was a symbolic representative of England (a third type), even though descriptively he was a German. My argument is that similar considerations hold for the concept of political participation and that Putnam and Skocpol are studying one type of participation, while I have been studying another. Scholars must be clear about such distinctions and about the functions of the various types of political participation. Apparently I am a pioneer in applying Pitkin's argument about representation to participation, which is likely this book's major academic contribution.

I set forth this argument in a conference paper and sent it to my colleague Michele Micheletti in Sweden, who had been researching consumer boycotts against business, which I saw as one of the sorts of political participation I had called "creative participation." Michele suggested that we edit a book with chapters presenting still other forms of creative participation. Paradigm Publishers has just published that book, *Creative Participation: Responsibility-Taking in a Political World* (2010). Half the authors are European, and half are American.

Meanwhile I decided to expand my original paper into a short book, which would present examples of creative participation in four categories. First, the environment: This category reflects my research into the organization of public-interest lobbies and my opinion that the 200 (of 250) owners of condos in my building, following recycling practices, constitute a form of political participation (100 trips to the recycling bins per year, at 4 minutes each, times 200, constitutes 80,000 minutes of donated time). Second, political corruption: Having spent four weeks traveling in China, I focused on the importance of this country and noted that the 700 million rural Chinese are constantly protesting local-level corruption in spontaneous political action. Chinese rural protest struck me as having something in common with the 1890s communitywide anticorruption protests in the state of Wisconsin, an important predecessor to Robert La Follette's brand of Progressive reform. Third, political consumerism: A number of European political scientists have written about consumer protest using boycotts and other means, not relying upon government, to influence corporate practices. Political consumerism is also an American phenomenon, but up to now, there has been little social science writing in America about this type of creative participation. In my view, this lack of research is largely due to male (and possibly feminist) prejudice against housewives, who are not seen as having political potential. How many political scientists read the food pages in the *New York Times*? (I don't either.) To demonstrate political consumerism as worthy of serious study, I invited my graduate student, Catherine Griffiths, to demonstrate in an exploratory treatment that consumerism can be a serious topic for quantitative study as illustrated by survey data and graphical presentation. Fourth, globalization: Globalization is now a cliché; yet, it is absolutely true that citizens are increasingly motivated to public action when the entire planet is the frame of reference rather than just their own country. We can no longer restrict examination of interest groups and political participation to considering public action within just one single country.

As with my work on public-interest groups, I am not claiming that creative political participation is always the most important mode of participation. But if not always most important, it is still very important. We must all pay attention to creative political participation as a type of public action.

For this book, I am especially indebted to Michele Micheletti and Sultan Tepe for intellectual and moral support. Jean-Francois Godbout, Norma Moruzzi, and Karen Mossberger each made a helpful suggestion subsequently incorporated into the book.

I appreciate the support I received from Mary Beth Rose, Linda Vavra, and the Institute for the Humanities at the University of Illinois, Chicago (UIC), which provided funding for me to write most of this book. James Nell and Zach Gebhardt rescued me from word-processing glitches. I wish to thank Dick W. Simpson (head) and the Department of Political Science at UIC for granting released time to write the book.

CHAPTER 1

CREATIVE PARTICIPATION AND CIVIC INNOVATION

During these times, individual citizens find political participation increasingly paradoxical. Traditionally both citizens and political observers have thought of political participation in terms of such concepts as the Greek *agora* ("forum") in which the citizens of the polis met together to discuss and take action regarding political issues affecting the community. Or in the West they may have thought of political participation as taking action in pursuit of interests, which were then registered and aggregated by established institutions of political representation, the political participation of Robert A. Dahl's *Who Governs?* (1961). Yet, often the individual citizen finds him- or herself in the situation of one of the group of hunters in Jean-Jacques Rousseau's (1984) metaphor of the stag hunt. Rousseau posited just two hunters, but I will expand this to a group of hunters. The group of hunters seeks to stalk and surround a stag, to shoot it, and to divide up the prize venison. However, along the way the hunters constantly surprise numerous fat rabbits, an easy kill. The hunters must cooperate to pursue and surround the fleet stag, which they are not certain to accomplish. On the other hand, at any time, any one of the hunters can readily kill a rabbit and return home with meat for a nice meal, although not as desired as a slab of venison. As Rousseau notes, the hunters are caught in a paradox of participation. Each may himself be willing to reject a rabbit for the uncertain prospect of venison, but the individual hunter cannot be sure that all of the other hunters think the same way. If a single hunter shoots a rabbit, the stag, forewarned, will rush away at high speed, as will the other rabbits, except for the victim. Accordingly, the incentive for an individual hunter is to shoot a rabbit immediately before some other does and drives away all the other rabbits, let alone the stag. The individual thus settles for the sure acquisition of a smaller self-interest rather than cooperating with all the other individuals to obtain a much greater common good, stalking and surrounding the stag. And better to shoot a rabbit, before someone else does, thereby leaving the first individual with nothing at all—no rabbit, no stag. The individual is caught in a paradoxical system of participation in group action.

Rousseau's stag-hunt metaphor brilliantly foreshadows one of the central preoccupations of American social science during the last half century—the concern for dilemmas in gaining human cooperation, particularly in situations of imperfect communication. Cooperation dilemmas are frequently referred to as "prisoners' dilemmas" after a game-theory model parallel to Rousseau's stag hunt (Axelrod 2006). Two prisoners are held but separated, so they cannot communicate with each other. The jailors pressure each to confess and separately inform each prisoner of his situation. If both refuse to confess, both are set free. If both prisoners separately confess, each will get a moderate sentence. If one prisoner confesses, but the other refuses, the confessor will receive a light sentence, but the refuser will get a severe sentence. In this situation, one expects Rousseau's outcome: In order to avoid the worst (no rabbit, no stag), each prisoner will confess (get a rabbit) and will not cooperate for the best outcome (the stag). This is largely because each prisoner will expect the other prisoner to go for the rabbit; therefore, each prisoner will go for the rabbit rather than risk getting nothing at all (a severe sentence). And they cannot cooperate to get the best outcome. During the last half century, psychologists, sociologists, economists, and political scientists have built thousands of experiments and behavior models around the paradox of the prisoners' dilemma.

The late political economist Mancur Olson Jr. applied the idea of cooperation dilemmas to political behavior in *The Logic of Collective Action* (1965). Olson began with the basic economic concept of public goods, that is, goods that are jointly supplied and not appropriated by some agent (if one person in an area has the good, then all people have it). The basic example of a public good is clean air: If clean air is supplied to one person in an area, then all people in that area must have it. Olson's key observation is that many public policies of government provide public goods: national defense, safety from crime, systems of public health, a common monetary system, and so forth. Then Olson applied another key observation to interest-group behavior. If an interest group seeks a public good, or merely even a collective benefit, for everyone within the group, why should the individual contribute to the public action by the group if the individual will get the collective benefit regardless whether he participates? Still another Olsonian observation was that this problem is most likely to crop up if the group comprises numerous individuals (say more than one hundred). It will then seem to the individual that his contribution to public action makes little difference, and if the public action succeeds, the individual will get the collective benefit anyway. Of course it then follows that in such large group situations, it is not rational for any individual to contribute to the public action; hence, the public action will not occur, resulting in the lack of provision of some widely valued collective benefit. On the other hand, if just a few agencies, such as individuals or corporations, take interest in some public action, the few agents (say ten or fewer) are each likely to make their contribution because each contribution makes a difference, and each agent expects the few other agents to realize this; thus, all make the contribution to the public action, thereby providing the benefit to the small group. Then, however, the bottom line is that if we consider political participation to be the aggregation of interests by representative institutions, the few will defeat the many because this logic of collective action holds that the few will engage in public action while the many will not participate in public action. Or in everyday language, the special interest will defeat the public interest.

Let us examine the situation of individuals caught within these paradoxical systems of action without communication: the stag hunt, the prisoner's dilemma, the logic of collective action. In such dysfunctional systems, individuals may prefer to cooperate, but they cannot cooperate without being able to communicate. In chasing the stag, the hunters are scattered through the forest. The prisoners are purposely held in separate cells. In the logic of collective action, the costs involved for one individual to communicate with hundreds or even thousands or millions are ordinarily too prohibitive for the individual to act. I refer to individuals caught in these dilemmas of cooperation without communication as "scattered."

A second aspect of the situation of the scattered individuals caught in these paradoxical systems of action is that they are frequently seeking to cooperate to attain a common good. The hunters seek to cooperate to surround and kill the stag. The isolated prisoners seek to be set free. The scattered individuals in Olson's logic of collective action seek to gain a "collective benefit" or "public good." In such situations, systems blocking communication frustrate individuals' desire to cooperate to attain a common or public good. True, Olson's collective-action paradox also applies to systems of organizing more than one hundred units that may be seeking a particular interest, as when hundreds of small businesses (say bakeries) seek to form a trade association to lobby for a given benefit. But Olson's paradox applies most poignantly to democratic theory in situations in which the diffused interests of millions of scattered citizens cannot be organized, as in the case of millions damaged by pollution or suffering a monopolistic price increase. I refer to such individuals as seeking *commonweal* goals, in respect to the language of seventeenth-century American colonists and to avoid the greater moralistic shading of phases like "the common good" or "the public interest."

A third characteristic of these paradoxes blocking common action is that *no established political institutions* exist to coordinate cooperation among the scattered individuals seeking the commonweal. One could imagine in the stag-hunt example that there might be institutional coordination, as when all the hunters are soldiers under the command of a leader, to forewarn them against shooting a rabbit. One could imagine that the prisoners, rather than being criminals rejecting the laws, could again be soldiers, each expecting the other to follow previous instructions given in training (e.g., do not confess). The perhaps millions of scattered individuals caught in Olson's logic of collective action cannot form an interest group to lobby the legislature for their collective benefit. In fact, the political philosophy of liberalism argues that the activities of the state must solve the paradoxes of seeking the commonweal. Such philosophical liberals (in the European sense) are critical of the need for an expansive state but grant the need for the state to act to coordinate cooperation when paradoxes of action block private individuals from acting to attain the commonweal. Nineteenth-century classical economics and its successors therefore grant the need for the state to provide "public goods" when they cannot be attained through private cooperation (Olson 1965, 102). Christian, Muslim, Aristotelian, Marxist, and other theories of the state normally do accept the need for established political institutions to act to coordinate cooperation for the commonweal but regard paradoxes of participation as arguments secondary to other ethical foundations for the state.

Creative Political Participation

Sometimes scattered individuals seeking public action toward a commonweal goal but, lacking established political institutions to pursue that goal, must engage in *creative political participation*. The scattered individuals must then create some new vehicle for cooperation to undo the system of scattering—the logic of collective action or the various barriers to communication causing dilemmas of cooperation. Native American hunters coordinated the pursuit by communicating through animal cries; American military prisoners held by the North Vietnamese communicated through a system of tapping on cell walls; environmentalists and corruption opponents overcame the logic of collective action around 1970 by devising systems of entrepreneurial organization employing direct-mail technology. Subsequently, through the 1970s and 1980s, direct-mail-based public-interest groups established themselves as a new institution for political participation among scattered citizens seeking commonweal goals (Bosso 2005; McFarland 1984). Other types of creative participation for commonweal goals include the formation of transnational advocacy networks, transcending the established boundaries of national organizations, and engaging in boycotts and other actions against current policies of major business corporations (Keck and Sikkink 1998; Micheletti 2003).

Scholars need to pay additional attention to *creative participation as civic innovation*. This parallels the difference between Olson's collective benefits and the traditional economics concept of public goods. As noted, a rather large group of scattered agents (individuals or businesses) will have difficulty mobilizing its collectivity into a lobby to pursue a common group interest or collective benefit. However, that benefit may be a special interest, such as organizing sugar growers to get import quotas that increase the price of sugar. On the other hand, there are public goods or collective benefits that benefit almost everyone within some defined area. The most famous public good is clean air, one of many such environmental public goods.

I use the phrase "civic innovation" to refer to creative participation to organize new modes of cooperation to obtain a public good, a benefit for everyone within some civic boundary. From the standpoint of the planet as a whole, civic innovation includes initiating new forms of public action transcending national boundaries and seeking the commonweal of the entire planet. Some people at least part of the time regard *civitas* as pertaining to the entire world.

The concept of political participation resembles that of representation as presented by political philosopher Hanna Fenichel Pitkin (1967) in a work that has met consensual acceptance by political scientists. Pitkin pointed out that there are several separable uses of "representation"; for instance, when George I of Hanover was imported to be the British monarch, one might say that he was not "descriptively representative" of the British because he was German and did not speak English. On the other hand, upon becoming the monarch, George I was "symbolically representative" of the British as the wearer of the crown and a descendant of William the Conqueror and the Tudor Henry VII. After differentiating several concepts of representation, Pitkin showed that they should not be confused with one another but might adhere together in some political situation. A similar observation can be made about the concept of political participation as illustrated below.

Different Concepts of Political Participation

I refer to the situations of the stag hunt, the prisoners' dilemma, and the logic of collective actions as paradoxes of political participation because we have in mind other situations in which there are few such dilemmas for cooperation in public action. The first such traditional form of action and political idea is the *political forum* or the *agora* (the marketplace). The classical civilizations of Athens and Rome valued political participation by the entire citizenry (a restricted group) in the central forum or marketplace to discuss jointly political issues affecting the citizenry with the goal of establishing common action, coordinated by leaders representing the citizenry. This is the forum model of political participation (Arendt 1998; Pateman 1970). It has played a central role in the humanities since the Renaissance. In the United States, the forum model was joined by the similar town-meeting model in which the farmers and merchants of a New England township would meet together, discuss issues, and elect the board of selectmen. In both academic and everyday political heritage, we regard the political forum as an institution furthering political participation (Mansbridge 1983).

A second model of political participation I term the *interests-and-institutions* (I&I) model. This form of political activity, and the modeling of it, is most familiar to the American citizen. This is the political participation referenced by classical liberal political theory. Citizens are seen as individuals who act in politics to express and further their own interests. The political system incorporates a set of institutions that register and aggregate the individual interests as they are expressed in action within the context of the aggregative institutions. There are four basic forms of political participation within the I&I model (Verba and Nie 1972; Verba, Schlozman, and Brady 1995, added movement protest). The first is expression of interest in the institution of elections through voting. The second is expression of interest through campaigning for representatives in the system of elections. The third is expression of individual interest through joining or contributing to an interest group and lobbying or petitioning government institutions on behalf of its individual interests. Olson, of course, said that such participation was ineffective in representing the interests of large groups. Finally, within the I&I model, the individual citizen may directly contact a governmental official to express an interest and get that official to act to consummate it. Unlike the forum model, the I&I model in its basic form does not concern itself with the value of widespread public discussion of issues. This I&I model is excellently expressed in Dahl's 1961 classic *Who Governs?*

A third form of social and political participation is civic engagement (Putnam 2000). This concept emphasizes the importance of face-to-face social interaction in building the trust necessary for humans to cooperate in social institutions. The extent of trust is referred to as "social capital," a well-iterated term in recent social science. Individuals are viewed as engaged in social and civic interaction and thereby contributing to the social capital necessary to maintain the group structure of society. Alexis de Tocqueville, a classic author familiar to undergraduate political science and sociology majors for the last two generations, famously put forth this perspective in the 1830s. Robert Putnam (2000), author of the famous "bowling alone" analogy and criticism of social trends in America, recently sharpened and refined Tocqueville's social theory. In the widely known analogy, Putnam stated that in the 1950s, American bowlers participated in a face-to-face manner in communitywide bowling leagues; by the 1990s such leagues had largely disappeared, leaving bowlers to participate only in small groups of immediate family and friends. In general, Putnam chronicled the decline of neighborhood interactive groups, replaced by solitary activities such as watching television at home or longer and longer commutes to work. Putnam expressed concern for the effects of such trends on the quality of social interaction, particularly on the quality of social trust and of democracy built upon it. Civic engagement in Putnam's sense refers to face-to-face participation in social groups in general, including lodges, sports associations, political-party gatherings, parent-teacher associations, and so forth. Political participation in face-to-face groups is thus one type of the general social-participation concept, but it is a particularly important type of social participation within the work of civic-engagement theorists.

A fourth type of political and social participation is participation within social movements. The political sociology of social movements has advanced greatly since the 1970s, even though there is no agreement on the precise definition of "social movement" (McAdam 1999). A central tendency in delineating social movements is the use of noninstitutional tactics in the pursuit of movement goals. Such tactics might include nonviolent demonstrations, strikes, threats or the use of violence, consciousness-raising groups, disruption of transportation and commerce, and so forth. In the United States, social movements often simultaneously employ institutional tactics, such as litigation and lobbying of legislative bodies. Social movements are usually contrasted to other forms of collective behavior, ephemeral in nature, such as crowd behavior or social fashions and fads (Orum 2001, 225–226). Adherents to a social movement are defined as advocating a major change in social institutions, often accompanied by a redefinition of personal and group identity for the movement adherents.

Creative participation by definition springs from the lack of established political institutions; social-movement behavior by definition employs noninstitutional tactics and may itself create new institutions in opposition to the established institutions. In the creation of institutions, the two forms of participation overlap. While it is not explicitly accepted in the writings of all social-movement scholars, most seem to accede to Alberto Melucci's (1996) concept of a social movement as behavior based on "critical codes," thus fundamentally critical of one or more social institutions. As indicated below, creative participation may include political behavior that consciously defends the status quo of legitimate institutions, some of which are seen as having been hijacked by special-interest coalitions. In such cases, creative participation is supportive, rather than critical, of existing institutions. An example is environmental lobbies working to enforce existing environmental legislation passed by Congress.

Political movements may be seen as proceeding from the organization of cooperation among scattered participants, as occurs in creative participation. However, most political movements constitute a statement of redefinition of group and personal identity. This is not the case with creative participation, which focuses instead on cooperating in pursuit of commonweal goals. However, some political movements, such as environmentalism, pursue more than the interests of a single group and, as such, their activities overlap with the concept of creative participation. In local instances, we might be reluctant to speak of political-movement participation, as when, for instance, dozens of local governments in the Los Angeles basin cooperate to maintain the water in an aquifer (Ostrom 1990, ch. 4). In this chapter, I refer to *political*, not *social*, movements, as a few social movements are not especially political, such as the American Protestant evangelism of the 1930s and 1940s, which eschewed political activity (Wilcox 1992, 7–8).

Thus, I regard creative participation as a fifth form of participation supplementing the previous discussions of the forum, I&I, civic engagement, and social movements. My sense is that creative participation is not as frequent a phenomenon as the others, excepting the forum. However, it may be that with globalization phenomena, creative participation is becoming more frequent, as individuals come to care more about the environmental and human rights policies of countries other than that of their own residence. Creative participation also derives significance in that it is rooted in universal dilemmas of human cooperation, as symbolized by the stag hunt, the prisoners' dilemma, and Olson's logic of collective action.

One virtue of delineating separate forms of political participation is the avoidance of needless scholarly controversy. As an analogy to Pitkin's work, there is no point to arguing that "true" representation is that of the principle and his agent, or the symbolic representation of the monarch or the president, or the descriptive representation of the organizational board that must contain 50 percent women. Similarly, there is no point to arguing that "true" participation is one or the other of the five forms just described. Dahl did regard I&I as participation in *Who Governs?* and was met with famous criticism from Carole Pateman (1970), who argued that political participation also includes discussion of issues presented to a group. By now most scholars recognize both as different types of participation, which some hope to bring together in a theory of "deliberative democracy" (Fishkin 1992). Since 1995, there has been enormous interest in the theory of civic engagement, and now the issue is whether civic-engagement writers might downgrade and refuse to discuss creative participation that does not include face-to-face interaction. Civic-engagement theorists should not eliminate public-interest lobbies, transnational advocacy networks, and consumer boycotts from the realm of significant public action.

Table 1.1 contrasts the five types of political participation. As stated, creative participation sometimes appears in contexts in which scattered individuals, seeking commonweal goals, lack established political institutions to engage in public action toward these goals. Scattering refers to a lack of communication impeding cooperation or to Olson's point about the difficulties of organizing a large number of individuals to form a lobby to attain a collective benefit or commonweal goal. Scattered individuals are not in engaged in face-to-face interaction.

In the context of the forum model of participation, there is no scattering; citizens meet in a specific place. The citizens are concerned with commonweal goals and discussing issues affecting them jointly; the meeting is an established

Table 1.1 Types of Political Participation

	Forum	Interests & Institutions	Civic Engagement	Social Movements	Creative Participation
Scattered people	Low	Medium	Low	Low	High
Commonweal goals	High	Low/medium	Medium	Low	High
Established institutions	High	High	High	Low/medium	Low

political institution. In the context of I&I, expressed in one form by *Who Governs?*, scattering is medium; citizens do not meet face-to-face in voting, the most important participatory institution; they do meet face-to-face in campaign and interest-group meetings. Commonweal goals are low/medium, indicating that in strict liberal models (in the European sense) of I&I, individuals are seen to be pursuing their own interests. However, as applied in empirical political science, the I&I model includes citizens making sincere commonweal claims in advocating policies, such as urban renewal in *Who Governs?*, seen to be good for the city as a whole (although not for those individuals who were removed). The model by definition treats political participation as a matter of citizens expressing individual interests within a system of political institutions that represents and aggregates.

The civic-engagement model of participation by definition emphasizes face-to-face interaction. While engagement focuses on the development of commonality among individuals, this commonality usually entails a particular group acting in cooperation rather than for a community as a whole. Nevertheless, participation can sometimes be for a commonweal goal of a community (usually a locality). By definition, individuals are civically engaged in established institutions. The political-movement model of participation ordinarily sees individuals as scattered, then mobilized into a movement in which they cooperate toward a goal. Normally political movements concern group identity, group rights in a society, and possibly economic position. However, a few political movements concern commonweal goals, such as environmentalism. In this case, the political-movement model overlaps with the creative-participation model. By definition, political movements reject at least some established political institutions.

The political forum, I&I, civic engagement, and political movements are all established, significant models (or perhaps categories) for political analysis. They are separate but frequently linked in political analysis. Civic engagement provides a basis for the forum and for some of the institutions in pluralist mechanisms. Especially in the United States, some political-movement participants organize lobbying groups that become institutionalized. Similarly, creative participation is sometimes linked to political behaviors reflecting the other models. In particular, new modes of expressing commonweal goals may become institutionalized as lobbies or even political parties (green parties). As noted, creative participation is sometimes closely linked to, or overlaps with, political-movement participation, especially in the case of environmentally concerned individuals acting in new ways to further commonweal goals.

To explore further the meaning of creative participation and civic innovation, in the remainder of this chapter we look at five important arenas of action for this type of political participation: diffused interests and the logic of collective action, implementation of public policies, opposition to political corruption, political consumerism, and transnational advocacy networks. These areas caught my attention as exhibiting creative participation while I conducted previous writing and research. In this book I aim simply to persuade the reader that something like creative participation exists in politics. I do not have the intention of scientifically delineating the "universe" of creative participation.

Diffused Interests and the Logic of Collective Action

The logic of collective action means that public policies are public goods—if one citizen receives a benefit, such as an improvement in the environment, then all citizens also benefit by the very nature of the public good. However, individuals are modeled as self-interested, mostly in respect to material goods, although sometimes in regard to solidary (friendship) benefits. It follows that self-interested individuals do not contribute to political efforts to gain a public policy that produces a public good because they will receive the same good even if they do not contribute. This is the famous concept of the free rider. A small group of agents, corporations, professional associations, or entrepreneurs, however, will find it in their particular interest to fund a lobby since the benefits to each outweigh the costs. Accordingly, special-interest lobbies will organize, but public-interest lobbies will not due to the costs of cooperation. The result is a serious limitation upon the possibilities of democratic government (Olson 1965).

Of course, I have assumed that some citizens, some of the time, exhibit civic virtue and desire to act, not out of self-interest but out of a desire to attain the commonweal for the entire citizenry in some area of public action. This is a way of explaining why so many lobbies exist despite the logic of collective action. Nevertheless, most social scientists would agree that self-interest is nonetheless an extremely widespread motivation and that consequently joint public action in the pursuit of public goods is frequently very difficult. Hence, minority interests tend to rule, and democratic governance is limited.

A major theoretical argument and empirical finding in public-policy studies is that the costs of organizing collective action by the many lead to control by the few particularistic coalitions of interest groups, legislators, and enforcement agencies controlling a public-policy area in which they have a stake. In the vernacular, this is known as the power of "iron triangles" or "special-interest" rule. Many political scientists have argued that this produces a major limitation on democratic governance, as noted in such famous works as E. E. Schattsch-neider's *The Semisovereign People* (1960), Grant McConnell's *Private Power and American Democracy* (1966), and Theodore Lowi's *The End of Liberalism* (1979). The solutions each proposed to enhance democratic government in the United States are familiar: national political parties with clear and differing issue platforms able to implement these platforms in Congress (Schattschneider); the New Deal image of a strong president and Supreme Court, backed by a national political party, advocating the interests of the popular majority (McConnell); a Congress enacting legislation giving clear administrative direction with a Supreme Court insisting that Congress not delegate decisions to administra-tors controlled by interest groups (Lowi). However, recent events indicate that such political institutional changes may work more to the interests of business than those of a general public. After the Gingrich election of 1994 up to the 2006 elections, the national Republican Party had a distinctively pro-business agenda and, by attaining majorities in both houses of Congress or by executive orders, was able to enact much of that agenda, which was increasingly backed by the Supreme Court and other federal courts. Environmental, consumer, and government reform interests were set back in the institutional logic of stronger political parties, a centralized executive branch under the president, and decisive enactments by federal courts.

However, civic innovation has been powerful in the arenas of the collective-action paradox. Described by both Putnam and Skocpol as not a manifestation of civic engagement (Putnam 2000, 152–161; Skocpol 2004), environmental, consumer, and good-government lobbies formed by direct-mail solicitation, later supplemented by e-mail, have resulted in the exercise of a significant degree of countervailing power to special-interest coalitions. A considerable amount of research has demonstrated this (Walker 1991; Rothenberg 1992; Berry 1999; McFarland 2004; Bosso 2005). The new public-interest lobbies are not participatory to any great extent—one normally expects only 3 to 5 percent of contributors to do anything more than write a check. Such groups also often do not have local chapters, or if they do, they embody only a small fraction of contributors. Such public-interest lobbies are based on the idea of efficient representation through contributions to professional representatives, either lobbyists or public-relations professionals (Bosso 2005).

But it is not in the nature of ordinary language to argue that contributions to political representatives are not participation—this is merely a form of participation different from face-to-face social engagement, public discussion of common issues, or self-interested action through existing institutions. Instead, innovative participants have created public-interest lobbies to deal with the political situation of a widespread concern to rectify social injustice in some area, when such a concern is shared by many citizens scattered about with no immediate institutional recourse. The logic of collective action points to a significant limitation upon democratic governance, but participation in civic innovation has helped to counter the marked imbalances in the process of interest mobilization.

Policy theorist Hugh Heclo noted that influential elites in separate issue areas form "issue networks," separable by particular policy areas. The issue network is the observable communications network of those actively attempting to influence policy in some area, although some academics and journalists limit themselves to framing issues and analyzing policy alternatives. An issue network comprises individuals from all sorts of interest groups, including public-interest groups, concerned with policy in an area, as well as politicians, legislative staff, executive branch officials, state and local government personnel, academic researchers, journalists, celebrities, and individual active concerned citizens. Issue-area participants communicate through public-relations statements, legislative hearings, periodicals, media reports, specialized media regarding the particular issue area, and telephone and e-mail communications among themselves. Issues regarding common policy for the entire citizenry are often discussed, not as in the forum model but sequentially among varying clusters of issue-network participants. Issue-area participants will sometimes meet face-to-face at professional conferences regarding their particular issue (Heclo 1978).

Participation in issue networks is a form of creative participation, or a type of participation close to that. Issue networks embody scattered participants who generally communicate through media, now particularly electronic media, especially e-mail. Participation in issue networks is normally not face-to-face, although subgroups of individuals within the network do have annual conventions. Many participants within an issue network seek to advance their own interests, and this is not creative participation. For instance, within the issue network concerning regulation of air pollution, electric utilities will seek to slow or redefine regulations to maintain business profits. On the other hand, many participants within the issue network seek the commonweal, such as scientists, environmental advocates, and public health professionals participating within the air-pollution-regulation network. This is a type of creative participation, as normally such individuals engage not in face-to-face discussion but in communication through electronic media. It is stretching the idea of "institution" to refer to an issue network as one, since an issue network does not have stable borders or constant participation by the same individuals who may come and go, as their participatory motives change over periods of several years.

Issue-network participation is an elite phenomenon, although participants may in some sense represent constituencies, such as an interest group. Heclo originally stated the issue-network concept as providing a major check upon the unbridled power of issue-area oligopolies, which might be considered unchecked due to the logic of collective action. As the site of framing of public issues eventually discussed by legislatures, issue networks have power over the agenda. They sometimes form the basis for the organization of ad hoc lobbying coalitions, some of which seek to represent widespread interests to counter oligopolistic coalitions. Such communication processes are not civic engagement in that they are restricted to a small number of people. On the other hand, the innovative creation of issue networks, along with the organization of public-interest lobbies, has proven a significant limitation to the concept of the few necessarily defeating the many in the control of policy issues.

Implementation Policies

As a study, policy implementation gets less than its share of intellectual respect. What happens after a bill becomes a law? Does anything much happen at all? As used in the American political science profession, "policy implementation" refers to much of public administration but, by convention, focuses on administrative action while relegating the social science study of organizations, bureaucracy, and government personnel to examination under other categories. Even so, policy-implementation studies are important to understanding what in fact actually happens in public action beyond the realm of law-setting discourse. The term first came into broad use in political science to refer to studies of why the domestic policies of the Lyndon Johnson administration largely failed to achieve their intended effects. Within political science, policy-implementation studies for the first time received major attention between 1970 and 1985; thereafter they received less attention as researchers concluded that the main variables in implementation behavior are understood (Pressman and Wildavsky 1973; Mazmanian and Sabatier 1989).

Students of political participation seldom refer to policy implementation as a realm for public action. But, to reiterate its significance, implementation is not just a study of what went wrong in the administration of Great Society programs. Implementation concerns also apply to the policies of Republican administrations as illustrated by two examples. The Ronald Reagan administration's immigration bill of 1986 had a major impact in legalizing perhaps 2.7 million illegal immigrants—a policy effectively implemented. But the bill had virtually no impact in its attempt to control illegal immigration through the regulation of hiring by private employers. Due to the complexity of undertaking such regulation and the political resistance by employers, such hiring regulation was conducted only at a token level. In effect, half of this major bill was repealed during the implementation process. A second example is the G. W. Bush regime's "No Child Left Behind" education policy, which has undergone great difficulty during the implementation process; it remains to be seen whether this major legislation will have significant impact upon the conduct of public education. Actually, during the 1960s political elites understood there was an issue about poverty programs being effectively implemented to aid the poor, as opposed to being redefined by government welfare bureaucracies (Piven and Cloward 1977). Accordingly, clauses stipulating "maximum feasible participation" were inserted into federal urban community–development measures, but the resulting participation in policy implementation was widely regarded as ineffective (Moynihan 1969; Lowi 1979).

Implementation participation may be in the category of civic-innovative participation if there is widespread but scattered concern that implementation is unjust in not following the original legislative intent. No established institutions may exist to facilitate the protest of such concerns about injustice. Consequently, innovative participation may involve issue networks, advocacy coalitions, and public-interest lobbies. Many participant communicators in a policy network may be concerned about unjust policy implementation. They might only contact legislators or executive officials, a standard type of participation (Verba, Schlozman, and Brady 1995). But they might also form communications links among themselves to form an issue or advocacy coalition. An issue coalition is defined as a relatively short-lived (say two years or less) political coalition to influence change in some policy area, including to enforce policy implementation as intended by the original legislation. The concept of advocacy coalition (Sabatier and Jenkins-Smith 1993) refers to a wide coalition among political elites, lasting for a substantial length of time (say ten years). The efforts of such a coalition are likely to include political and legal efforts to implement legislation as the coalition prefers; for example, a clean-air coalition might monitor the policies of the Environmental Protection Agency. Most participants in an advocacy coalition also participate in an issue network, which acts as a communication network for recruitment to advocacy coalitions. Of course, a general issue network may include within itself both pro and anti advocacy coalitions regarding a specific issue.

Public-interest lobbies, examples of civic innovation, often spend much of their time monitoring policy implementation and seeking to shape it via litigation and getting critical messages to the media. Environmental issues provide many such examples. Common Cause will monitor policies of the Federal Elections Commission regarding campaign-finance legislation. Implementation policy in general overlaps with collective-action issues, although it obviously does not encompass all such issues. As expressed in issue networks, advocacy coalitions, and public-interest groups, implementation politics is another arena for innovative participation.

Political Corruption

A third domain for civic-innovative participation is action against political corruption. Corruption has been defined generally as "the misuse of public power for private gain" by Rasma Karklins, a leading scholar of the subject, who notes, "When talking about corruption, people often think only of bribery, but it exists in many other forms, such as extortion, profiteering from procurement, and institutional capture. These often involve the accessory acts of fraud, dereliction of duty, and the violation of multiple laws. Corrupt privatization or procurement deals tend to include collusion or blackmail and the corruption of others, including legislators or journalists" (2005, 5, 19). Political corruption is a major factor impeding democratic governance and economic development, particularly in the Third World and formerly Communist nation-states.

Whether in contemporary China, Russia, or Nigeria or in the Los Angeles water and power district of the film *Chinatown*, individuals opposing corruption are often scattered, experience a concern about civic injustice more than one for personal self-interest, and face a lack of established political institutions to express their desire for justice, especially as the corrupted individuals themselves quite possibly control the established political institutions. This, then, is the situation of civic innovation.

The major issue about political corruption is systemic corruption—the situation in which everyone converts the public into the private, expects everyone else to take bribes for government service and contracts, and so forth (Karklins 2005). Honest citizens, stuck in such a system and wishing to change it, are subject to the cooperation dilemma of the logic of collective action. Such honest citizens may be isolated and alone. Where are the other honest citizens, each may wonder. Here, any form of action is civic-innovative participation, even the decision to follow the law within a system of action in which lawbreaking is the norm. Other forms of participation do not apply: There is no public forum of debate because the public forum is broken into parts that are then controlled by individuals. Established mechanisms of interests/institutions are themselves the source of injustice. Civic engagement when the system is corrupt is engagement in corruption; individuals learn to trust one another to be lawbreakers in common. Today, this systemic corruption is a common problem in post-Communist societies.

I do not imply that forming something like a public-interest lobby is the only means to fight corruption. Karklins states, "The three cornerstones of corruption containment are creating institutional checks and balances, assuring that the mechanisms of accountability actually work, and mobilizing the citizenry to participate in enhancing the public good" (2005, 163). Elections can bring to power a new government with anticorruption goals; this has been demonstrated in Turkey and Palestine, where secular governments, widely viewed as corrupt, were replaced in elections by Islamic leaders, seen to be more honest. On the other hand, fighting corruption sometimes involves the innovative participation of forming a public-interest group and enhancing it with an advocacy coalition, as Karklins reports happened once in Latvia: "In spring 2002 Transparency International–Latvia led a grassroots campaign against a suspect effort to privatize a youth sports and recreation facility.... The breakthrough came when TI–Latvia garnered the support of fifty-eight other nongovernmental groups and thousands of individuals who signed appeals" (2005, 159).

Views of corruption obviously vary with social norms, as in the famous statement attributed to an Irish American Tammany politician: "I seen my opportunities and I took 'em" (Riordan 1963, 3). In the United States, Common Cause and other such groups oppose practices for which the term "corruption" seems a bit strong: private interests legally pouring money into political campaigns, legislators being paid for additional work by nongovernmental sources, closed meetings by government officials, and so forth. However, such practices do have the potential to become the vehicles for corrupt practices.

Political corruption produces a disintegration of democratic governance. In systems of corruption, honest citizens must engage in civic-innovative participation.

Transnational Political Activism

Individuals may be scattered, without established institutions to engage in action regarding perceived injustices within foreign countries. Before processes of innovative participation are initiated, the citizens' government may have no interest at all in some foreign injustice, or at first transnational advocacy networks may not be organized to facilitate public action (Keck and Sikkink 1998). Public policy making can be described as a matter of the politics of attention and what gets priority attention from governments (Jones and Baumgartner 2005); at first a government may have no concern about such questions as human rights violations in Darfur or the shrinking of the Brazilian rain forest. To reiterate, here I am concerned with participation in matters regarding events in foreign countries, not the institutionalized participation occurring as citizens attempt to influence the foreign policy of their own governments.

Although one suspects that the processes of globalization increase the concern of individuals for events in foreign countries, we must note that transnational participation is not a new phenomenon. An international abolitionist movement existed in regard to slavery everywhere, including the British Empire; especially before World War I, socialists proclaimed their international identification with, and concern for, the working class in all modern countries; in 1936 to 1939 leftists without regard to their own governments' policies participated in

Republican resistance to Franco in the Spanish Civil War. In the last generation, however, the number of transnational political organizations has increased. Sociologist Jackie G. Smith counted an increase in nongovernmental international social-change organizations from 183 in 1973 to 631 in 1993, with an amazing increase in international environmental organizations from 10 in 1973 to 90 in 1993 (Keck and Sikkink 1998, 11). The overall trend has continued since 1993, subsequently enhanced by the availability of cheap e-mail communication for international coordination. Apparently most of this activity parallels that of domestic American public-interest lobbies; the transnational groups frequently consist of multinational staffs who appeal to a transnational constituency, often using the Internet, for financial contributions and various other types of support, such as signing petitions or contacting domestic legislators. This is not civic engagement, debating issues in a forum, or, at least initially, activism within established political institutions. Nevertheless, creative participation in transnational advocacy networks can be linked to the other forms of participation in some significant instances. In recent years, the most famous instance was the impact of transnational advocacy networks upon domestic political organizations concerning apartheid in South Africa before 1989. National legislatures in the United States, United Kingdom, and France, among others, took up the antiapartheid cause by supporting boycotts of South African products. Creative participation in this case had a major effect on institutional foreign policy (Klotz 1995). Another form of creative participation in the international arena is the organization of "social forums," international meetings of thousands of antiglobalization activists, complete with panels and speakers for the presentation and discussion of international issues. Such forums, however, are partially organized through the artifices of innovative participation, particularly the coordination of the meetings by ad hoc committees using the Internet. It is hard to link civic engagement to transnational advocacy networks, but the social forums do provide a limited means for what might be termed "transnational engagement," the building of trust among citizens of various countries (della Porta 2007, 60–61, 171–172, 223–224).

Participants in transnational advocacy networks often work together, but they also separately try to influence their own civic process to get various foreign ministries, agencies of the United Nations, or other international organizations to influence some third country to stop some practice seen as unjust, perhaps in the human rights or environmental areas. Scholars Margaret E. Keck and Kathryn Sikkink (1998, 12–13) have termed this the boomerang effect, as political action moves in a first direction, to one's own government, then moves in a second direction, from that government to another government whose policies are the actual object of concern. Participation in such international "boomerang politics" is apparently different from participation in discussion, mobilization of interests, or civic engagement related to domestic public policy making.

Transnational advocacy networks are a form of civic-innovative participation, even when they are immediately oriented to correction of unjust treatment of some group, such as women or sweatshop workers, in a foreign country as opposed to unjust civil rights violations or unjust depredations upon everyone's environment. In transnational situations, citizens of one country see as unjust the lack of established institutions to protest injustice in another country (Young 2006). The international framework of bounded nations itself seems unjust. In this situation, civic innovators have created new advocacy networks to influence their own and other governments.

Some observers might prefer to classify most transnational activism as a form of social-movement activity, but this would be a specific subtype of social movement, those not accepting preexisting national boundaries as the arenas framing the issues of protest.

Political Consumerism

Consumer purchasing decisions can be another form of innovative participation. Some consumers, at least some of the time, in addition to economic criteria use political criteria in buying goods and services. The universe of such decisions can be termed "political consumerism" (Micheletti 2003; Micheletti, Follesdal, and Stolle 2004). Here I focus more especially on situations in which scattered consumers, also acting as citizens, are concerned with some injustice to all citizens, or at least about some interests other than their own; they do not, however, act to express this concern through established political institutions but adapt their behavior in consumer purchasing. Such economic behavior is also political and may be a form of innovative participation.

Consumer boycotts of British tea and other goods preceded the American Revolution. Mahatma Gandhi's boycott of British salt and textiles was a high point in twentieth-century political history. The U.S. civil rights movement featured scores of local boycotts by blacks against segregated businesses; this was political consumerism, as well as arguably both a social movement and civic innovation, in the sense that it improved the quality of democracy for the entire community as segregation laws were no longer enforced. One might hypothesize that with the increasing globalization of commerce and the possibilities of the Internet as an organizational communication device, political consumerism as innovative participation will become more widespread throughout the world.

Political consumerism as civic-innovative participation can be a solitary act, a citizen's refusal to buy a product that he believes is manufactured by an unjust producer. If in some case such beliefs become widespread, there is the possibility of organizing a boycott, sometimes a practice of labor unions in contemporary America. On the other hand, some consumers may react positively and buy from a producer or merchandiser seen to favor a just cause, for instance, those who shop at Trader Joe's for fair-trade coffee. An important tactic of political consumerism is product labeling, for instance, in indicating a union-made product, which can be defined as an indicator of just versus exploitative wages. Recently the fair-trade label on coffee has been treated as a symbol of just treatment of Third World coffee growers and the stewardship of the tropical environment. Other labels are a facet of political consumerism but may be seen as an indicator of self-interest, such as the consumption of organic foods for one's health or avoiding high-calorie foods (Micheletti 2003, 149–154; Vogel 2005, 51–56; Holzer 2007; Wilkinson 2007).

Political consumerism often overlaps with transnational participation. The Nestlé boycott, for instance, was a consumerist action taken against a Swiss multinational corporation for the sake of the health of babies in the Third World. Recent actions have included boycotts of Nike and other shoe manufactures for paying low wages in Third World manufacturing and of Starbucks for not featuring fair-trade coffee. If an international boycott is an instrument of the foreign policy of nation-states, such as the American government's boycott of mainland China before 1972 or the 1950s Arab League boycott of companies doing business with Israel, it is not a category of individual participation.

Boycotts, buying campaigns, and labeling to express political goals are not examples of forum participation, mobilization of interest through established institutions (at least not at first), or civic engagement, as consumer decisions are conducted individually. However, political consumerism, as creative participation, is linked to these other forms of participation in that consumerism may increase civic engagement to a small degree (participating in boycott groups if such exist), and widespread consumerist sentiments may be organized and reinforced by labor unions and political parties.

Political consumerism can be a form of expressing a view of the good society. A consumer might refuse to shop at Walmart and prefer to shop at small stores because he or she believes in a society of Jeffersonian commerce. The shopper-citizen knows that his or her individual shopping decisions have little effect but nonetheless derives satisfaction from taking independent action to express a social opinion, even at some cost to economic self-interest.

Conclusion

One aspect of the human condition entails the paradoxes of participation. In a number of political situations, individuals are isolated from one another, and the structure of the situation prevents cooperative action to achieve a common benefit. Such paradoxical situations occur when numerous scattered individuals seek a commonweal goal, but no established political institution provides a means for joint action to achieve it. Political action in common can occur in this situation if individuals engage in creative participation and civic innovation by inventing new modes of public action. Creative participation is one of a set of five types of participation, none of which should be regarded as "true" participation. Creative participation may occur in combination with one of the other four types. The nature of creative participation can be explored in the contexts of representing the diffused interests in Olson's logic of collective action, in public action regarding policy implementation, in action to combat governmental corruption, in political consumerism, and in transnational advocacy. Social scientists and political philosophers have commented less about creative participation than they have about other forms of participation.

I do not maintain, however, that civic innovation is always progressive and majoritarian. For instance, according to a colleague interviewing anti-immigration protestors, some see illegal immigration as unjust, lacking action from established institutions, and go about establishing their own border patrols and websites.

Although not always morally unblemished, civic innovation deserves attention simply for the reason that it is innovative. New modes of action are of interest to scholars and the general public. In addition, I suspect that public-interest lobbies, Internet-based communication and participation, transnational advocacy networks, and political consumerism are expanding their influence on politics.

A final conclusion is that scholars and public participants should investigate the balances among types of participation. The five types often bear some important relationship to one another. Civic engagement can provide the basis for civic concerns, beyond self-interest, to enhance political consumerism, which in turn, in some cases, might enhance civic engagement. Consumerism might sometimes lead to the creation of new public-interest lobbies, which, while not increasing civic engagement, would become established institutions to lobby government. Consumerism can provide new items for discussion of joint action on public policy, although unfortunately this is likely to be limited to elites participating in issue networks. Viewing the links among civic innovation and other forms of participation will enhance the understanding of the processes of public policy.

CHAPTER 2

THE ENVIRONMENT AND CREATIVE PARTICIPATION

Participation as civic innovation is defined in terms of scattered individuals—motivated by civic virtue, desiring public action to seek a commonweal goal (a good), and lacking established political institutions to do so—creating some new means of participation. Such civic innovation is commonly found in environmental politics because scattered citizens sometimes suffer environmental degradation jointly, but established political institutions do not exist or are inactive. Many such scattered citizens may not actually experience the particular environmental degradation but regard the situation as unjust and desire to join with others in public action to rectify it.

The basic situation of innovative participation for the environmental commonweal is developed below in terms of a number of concepts. First, we consider Mancur Olson Jr.'s well-known *The Logic of Collective Action* (1965), in which he posits that in a self-interest model, large groups lack participatory incentives because individuals are content to be "free riders," that is, to wait for others to participate in an action to establish a common good. The logic of collective action overlaps with the idea of "the tragedy of the commons," when there is no general incentive for collective action, leading to the destruction of a common-pool resource (Hardin and Baden 1977). The two ideas show the necessity of civic virtue and innovative participation for common action to protect the environment.

The general social science literature (as opposed to the study of public administration) neglects the importance of policy implementation. This relates to problems in establishing collective action for public goods because, even if civic-virtue motivations and civic participation establish governmental policy or private cooperation to provide the environmental good, citizens may withdraw their participation to defend the public good against the interests and actions of oligopolistic cliques, who seek to turn public policy into private profit. Effective policy implementation requires innovative civic participation.

Olson's logic of collective action concludes with the observation that the few defeat the many, as the few will organize lobbies, while the many will not. This ties into policy implementation, as "iron-triangle" coalitions of economic producers, government officials, and lobbyists will undermine public action for environmental goods for the sake of private profit (McConnell 1966; Lowi 1979). Collective action dilemmas and implementation politics have in the United States led to the formation of environmental lobbies, entailing civic innovation in the form of checkbook contributions providing the necessary resources for environmental lobbyists (Bosso 2005).

Public behavior for recycling solid wastes in Chicago is included as an example of civic innovation exhibiting civic-virtue motives in the wake of a failure in policy implementation. Individual motives to recycle are construed as an example of political participation.

The irony is that while initially political and state institutions were lacking in many environmental fields, public participation as civic innovation eventually bolstered the state by preventing special-interest cliques from converting public policy into private advantage.

Innovative Civic Participation: The Tragedy of the Commons

The widely known metaphor of the tragedy of the commons provides another important context for innovative civic participation. In short, those acting to prevent the "tragedy" engage in this type of participation, even when some might not call such actions political. Let us review biologist Garrett Hardin's classic definition:

> The tragedy of the commons develops in this way. Picture a pasture open to all. It is to be expected that each herdsmen will try to keep as many cattle as possible in the commons. Such an arrangement may work reasonably satisfactorily for centuries because tribal wars, poaching, and disease keep the numbers of both man and beast well below the carrying capacity of the land. Finally, however, comes the day of reckoning, that is, the day when the long-desired

goal of social stability becomes a reality. At this point, the inherent logic of the commons remorselessly generates tragedy.... As a rational being, each herdsman seeks to maximize his gain ... [and] concludes that the one sensible course for him to pursue is to add another animal to his herd. And another.... But this is the conclusion reached by each and every rational herdsman sharing a commons. Therein is the tragedy.... Freedom in a commons brings ruin to all. (1977, 20)

Olson's logic of collective action emphasizes the political problem of the few defeating the many, a problem for democracy. Hardin's tragedy may be restated as a dilemma of a lack of institutions to protect *common-pool resources*, in the words of Nobel Prize winner Elinor Ostrom (1990). The ideas overlap in that Olson would believe it unlikely for many self-interested individuals to find it in their interest to organize such an institution to protect public goods, unless the number of individuals were quite small. Everyone would wait for others to act, with all expecting to become free riders in the establishment of a policy to protect the commonweal.

Ostrom focuses the concept of the tragedy of the commons with her emphasis on the institutional problems in managing common-pool resources, such as the herdsmen's commons (cf. fish in a lake, etc.). Ostrom comments, "Standard analyses in modern resource economics conclude that where a number of users have access to a common-pool resource, the total of resource units withdrawn from the resource will be greater than the optimal economic level of withdrawal" (1990, 3). The term "common-pool resources" most clearly denotes things called "natural resources," such as water, land, fish, wildlife, and wilderness—things that are inherently limited in supply or, when the supply is drawn down by non-cooperative individuals, cannot easily be replenished. From a general ecology or sustainability standpoint, it sometimes makes sense to refer to a resource as a planetwide common-pool resource, viewing all of one thing on the planet as comprising a common pool, albeit partitioned into separate boundaries. For instance, pools of oil are separate from one another, but without some system of cooperation, we can expect individual producers to exploit separately owned oil pools as quickly as possible, leaving the overall planetary pool too diminished for further economic exploitation.

Accordingly, we can characterize individual motives as civic virtue if individuals, concerned about the diminution of common-pool resources, desire public action to preserve them. In this case, certain individual actions can be construed as "political" and contrasted with the other four models of political participation.

Individuals may devote some time to recycling household materials, for example, even though it is not in their immediate self-interest to do so (see discussion below). A recycling business, motivated more by desire to conserve planetary resources than by profit, is an instance of creative civic participation. An individual who rides a bicycle and gives up an automobile manifests civic virtue if the major motive is to preserve planetary common-pool resources of oil and iron (global warming is in a somewhat different category). In this case, riding the bicycle is an act of political participation. An individual who decides not to have children, persuaded by the concept of limited planetary resources, exhibits civic virtue, although of course the stated motive may not really be the primary motive.

Civic innovation would include actions by hunters and fishermen to voluntarily limit their kills in the interest of preserving the common-pool resource of game, very difficult to replenish beyond a certain point. Political action by hunters and fishermen to institutionalize such wildlife preservation is another strategy of civic innovation. In the 1920s in the United States, sportsmen (then largely men) established effective lobbies, such as Ducks Unlimited and the Izaak Walton League, to advocate for policies to police the hunting and fishing of wildlife (Bosso 2005, 27–33).

Of course, others in the United States besides hunters and fishermen established effective lobbies to preserve common-pool resources. Although it does not constitute civic-engagement participation, several million Americans send checks to a variety of lobbying organizations to support public action to preserve common-pool resources (Bosso 2005, 95–105). A smaller number, perhaps 3 to 5 percent of those mailing in contributions, do actually meet face-to-face in the activities of such environmental and ecological organizations (McFarland 1984, 101; Shaiko 1999, 146). Leading American organizations of this type include National Audubon Society, National Wildlife Federation, Ducks Unlimited, National Parks Conservation Association, The Nature Conservancy, World Wildlife Fund–US, American Rivers, Izaak Walton League, Natural Resources Defense Council, Defenders of Wildlife, The Wilderness Society, Trust for Public Land, National Park Trust, Conservation International, Rainforest Action, and the Clean Water Action, among others. In 2002, such organizations had substantial revenues: Nature Conservancy, $972.4 million for the tax-deductible purchase of land for conservation goals; Conservation International, $222.7 million, and Trust for Public Land, $126.5 million, for instance, in contributions largely from the wealthy and foundations. Other such groups had substantial revenues from member-contributors in 2002: Ducks Unlimited, $125.1 million; National

Wildlife Federation, $102.1 million; National Audubon Society, $78.6 million. Smaller amounts went to a number of lobbying organizations, such as $18.8 million for the Wilderness Society and $5.5 million for American Rivers. Such budgets serve as an index of civic virtue and active civic innovation (Bosso 2005, 97–98).

Garrett Hardin objects to how those who point to the possibilities of technological innovation to increase the level of the common pool avoid recognizing the tragedy of the commons. For instance, some might argue that the green revolution in agricultural production increased India's agricultural output, thereby staving off the tragedy. While Hardin (Hardin and Baden 1977) might prove right about the planet in the end, we can consider major efforts to increase the level of common-pool resources, or to use present common-pool resources more efficiently, or to create new types of such resources, as instances of creative civic participation.

Civic Participation and Policy Implementation

The logic of collective action and the tragedy of the commons sometimes are woven together to provide a context for innovative civic participation in public action regarding the environment. This context is quite complex and becomes even more so in relation to issues of policy implementation for environmental policy.

Dilemmas of cooperation in environmental policy can initially be surpassed, partly due to public action by citizens motivated by civic virtue. In the long run, however, it is often more important that environmental laws be implemented in the way intended by the initial lawgivers. Dilemmas of cooperation recur after public action is taken, and those motivated by civic virtue turn to private activity or to new public goals. With less support from civic innovators, there is a natural tendency for the state to be influenced, or even "captured," in a certain area by producers seeking to enhance profits by evading environmental laws. A recurrent case of the few defeating the many, as described by Olson's collective-action theory, may develop. Or perhaps the institution legislated to correct the tragedy of the commons will decay as people find loopholes allowing them to take common-pool resources. Without continuing political backup, including support from innovative participators, environmental policy tends to weaken.

Lack of a transnational aspect renders environmental situations even more complex, which is normally the case for important environmental issues. The environment is planetary, and issues such as global warming transcend the boundaries of particular nation-states. International conferences and separate national governments may legislate public action, but as with the Kyoto Conference, an equally important basis for public action lies in processes of policy implementation. The transnational environmental policy is highly complex, including scores of nation-states and shifting relationships regarding a common program among them. An incentive to rush to individual national enrichment undermines international agreements. This is clearly an important context for innovative civic participation, if we construe "civic" as regarding the commonweal of the entire planet as establishing political institutions and their necessary complexity are both part of the problem in achieving worldwide public action. Such transnational advocacy networks for the environment have become numerous, including both new and older national organizations that have expanded to include a transnational network. Well-known organizations within transnational environmental networks include Worldwide Wildlife Federation, Greenpeace International, and Rain Forest Action (Keck and Sikkink 1998).

But environmental policies in the domestic arena are complicated enough. Particularly between 1969 and 1974, the federal government passed a great deal of environmental legislation, such as the Clean Air Act of 1970, later amended in 1977 and 1990 (C. Jones 1975; McFarland 1993; Vogel 1989; Weidenbaum 1979). At this time, liberals controlled Congress, Richard Nixon did not resist the popular new environmental ideas, and business interests had not counterorganized to promote the argument that environmental regulation is inflationary and interferes with free markets (Orfield 1975). Strip-mining-control legislation was added during Jimmy Carter's administration and air-pollution regulation was extended. I would argue that the weight of environmental politics and policy at the federal level since 1981 has rested more on the politics of implementation on the passage of new laws; for example, there was virtually no support for the Kyoto Treaty in the Senate, so federal action about "global warming" concentrates on the implementation of air-pollution legislation as in the regulation of gasoline mileage of autos and trucks.

Granted that it is largely—or even somewhat—true, this picture of American national environmental policy provides a context of millions of scattered individuals, who favor the intent of the original law and vigorous law-regarding enforcement, becoming aware that in many instances the intent of the environmental law is being compromised. However, the expansion of existing environmental organizations in the 1969–1974 period, together with the founding of new environmental organizations then and later, provided an avenue for innovative civic participation (Walker 1991; Bosso 2005). In fact, by 1990 environmental lobbies had accumulated enough revenues, wealth, and skilled professional personnel that one could regard them as established political institutions (Bosso 2005). During this period, environmental lobbies had to become active in protesting compromises in the enforcement of the original legislation, for instance, by raising issues of the degree of regulation of auto and truck emissions and the need to refit older coal-burning electric plants with new air-pollution scrubbing equipment. However, in many cases environmental organizations had more difficulty organizing their political resources to gain the respectful attention of federal administrators in comparison to their significant influence in lobbying Congress. Lobbying the executive branch during pro-business presidential administrations is especially difficult. The near exclusion of environmental lobbies from Dick Cheney's energy-policy commission is a famous extreme case (Bosso 2005, 119). On the other hand, environmentalists achieved surprising success in lobbying Congress to maintain wilderness provisions governing the Alaska National Wildlife Reservation, even when the president, oil companies, and the residents of Alaska supported drilling for oil and Republicans controlled both congressional houses (Bosso 2005, 119–127).

The core action in supporting environmental lobbies consists of checkbook contributions, that is, individual citizens posting (and later e-mailing) contributions to support the lobbying effort in Washington, D.C. Apparently national environmental lobbies are supported by more than $1 billion per year in such checkbook contributions, not counting additional revenue received via larger contributions from foundations or corporate or wealthy individuals supporting efforts to buy land for conservation goals. Such contributions are not considered membership participation in the civic-engagement theory of participation. But the checkbook contributions enable lobbyists to have a critical impact, important in a discussion of participation as civic innovation (Bosso 2005; McFarland 1984, ch. 4; Rothenberg 1992).

As a category, lobbying on policy-implementation issues is not given much importance in social science literature; nor is the question of policy implementation in its entirety. Lawyers, on the other hand, discuss the effectiveness of legal language and legal texts and their relationship to law enforcement, a type of perspective on policy implementation. Students of public administration were particularly concerned about policy implementation following the failure to implement the goals of many of Lyndon Johnson's antipoverty and social welfare programs. But after identifying a number of factors apparently related to effective implementation, this public-administration discussion lapsed after the late 1980s (Pressman and Wildavsky 1973; Mazmanian and Sabatier 1989). Thus, since discussions of policy implementation in the social sciences have been regarded as a second-priority concern, participation on policy-administration issues have not received much comment. Consideration of such issues is a hallmark of the fifth category of political participation, civic innovation.

Recycling, Policy Implementation, and Participation

The policy of the city of Chicago toward recycling illustrates relationships among environmental policy, implementation issues, and civic participation. As is frequently the case with environmental issues at all levels of action, from the planetary to the urban, governments pass symbolic legislation for environmental protection, then do not implement it. The city of Chicago hauls away the waste from its several hundred thousand small residential buildings, but apartments and condominiums of more than four units contract with private haulers for waste management. In 1993, the city council and Mayor Richard Daley enacted the Chicago High Density Residential and Commercial Source Reduction Ordinance requiring multi-unit-building managers and their private waste haulers to set up programs to recycle at least three types of material. The law was known as the Burke-Hansen ordinance, after Alderman Edward Burke, a leading policy initiator after the powerful mayor, and Alderman Bernard Hansen, who represented a district containing many environmentally oriented young professionals, living in condos and apartments near the lake.

However, not for fourteen years, until 2007, was a serious move made to enforce the Burke-Hansen ordinance. Cook County commissioner Michael Quigley (elected to the U.S. Congress in 2009), who had helped write the ordinance in 1993 when he was an assistant to Alderman Hansen, noted in 2007, "No matter what happens with rewriting the law, they've got to enforce the damn thing" (Dumke 2007, 26). The city waited until 2004 to conduct inspections under the 1993 ordinance to see whether the law was being followed. For the period of November 2006 to September 2007, the city conducted 441 recycling inspections of businesses and issued them 106 citations. However, the city had yet to inspect any multiunit dwellings. Paul Ruesch, an environmental official, said, "Frankly, almost everyone ignores the law.... We just haven't had much luck in finding the political will to enforce the ordi-nances" (Dumke 2007, 26).

Nor was a second Burke-Hansen ordinance regarding multiunit-building recycling effectively implemented. Prior to 1993, another ordinance on the books allowed condo buildings to apply for a $75 rebate per unit since residents were paying taxes for the city's garbage pickup services, even though the condo was also paying for private haulers. Burke and Quigley amended the provision to require building managers to submit an affidavit of adoption of a recycling program to get the rebate. There was uneven enforcement of this provision, but the city allocated $6 million a year for such rebates, and the money ran out each year. Further, a building had to submit its notarized statement only once, and the recycling programs in some buildings likely lapsed, but the city would not know this since buildings were not inspected.

The city did not enforce the law regarding multiunit-building recycling ap-parently because of the expense of hiring inspectors and because some building managers (probably a minority) would consider this an excessive regulation. Further, the mayor seemed committed to a method of recycling for individual dwellings that involved throwing all recyclables into one blue bag for pickup by the city. The Burke-Hansen ordinance required separation of at least three types of material, implying that using one blue bag for recyclables was not a good idea. Many Chicagoans inferred that Mayor Daley did not like the implicit criticism of the program he initiated for the individual unit dwellers.

However, corresponding to increasing public interest in public action for the environment after the turn of the century, the city did start a small inspec-tion program for business recycling in 2004. In 2005, the city gave in a bit to environmental critics and started an experimental program in one ward out of fifty, giving single-unit residents the option of separating recyclables into four categories to be deposited in special carts left by the city in alleys. As environ-mental concerns continued to develop, in 2007 the city extended the four-bag program into six more wards due to vigorous appeals from several aldermen. One enthusiast was Alderman (Chicago women prefer this usage) Emma Mitts, representing an especially poor African American district. Another enthusiast, Alderman John Pope, represented an "ethnic" ward with many voters of Irish, Croatian, Serbian, and Mexican ancestry. It was no longer just the upper-middle-class professionals who pressed for environmental action (Dumke 2007).

I regard the Chicago recycling situation as a typical context for creative civic participation. It does not seem to matter where—be it at the transnational conference level, or the national level, or the city level, or in whatever country—environmental laws and regulations are propounded: frequently environmental legislation will not be implemented. In the Chicago case, it took ten years for environmentalists to achieve a start to enforcement of the multiunit recycling law. It may take another six or seven years to finally get effective implementation of it. In the Chicago example, one cannot point to a clear case of policy capture by some producer coalition, undermining policy for the sake of corporate profits.

Recycling activity by American citizens is an example of action springing from civic virtue, even if such action takes little effort and is quite pragmatic. Probably tens of millions of Americans now recycle household waste, even though they receive no specific reward or sanction for doing so. The effort seems minimal, but 5 minutes per week amounts to 260 minutes per year of donated time. Citizens acting in this way to establish recycling institutions is a case of innovative civic participation.

Do we want to call this *political participation*? In a discussion of innovative civic participation, I will do so. In the case of recycling, let us focus on the motive. Most of the millions who recycle do so because they consider it "the right thing to do" to preserve the common-pool resources of the nation and the planet. They see themselves as participating in a common effort, a public action for the commonweal. They do not behave as the tragedy of the commons predicts; they do not expect, nor is it very relevant to them, that millions of other citizens might not bother to recycle, thereby rendering their civic-virtue action meaningless.

Recycling would not be regarded as political participation in the terms of the other four categories of participation. Regarding the forum, the action of recycling is committed by the lone individual and thus does not really constitute political participation. Regarding participation as action to gain influence within the system of interest-aggregating institutions, one would not expect individuals to act due to the logic of collective action and the tragedy of the commons. In relation to civic engagement, again lone individuals or families conduct much recycling, and there is little face-to-face social interaction. True, such interaction may develop within the groups formed as part of civic-innovative participation. Recycling indicates the overlap between social-movement and creative participation but also shows the possibility of a separate category for the latter. Recycling does represent the assimilation of the norms of the previous environmental movement. However, present-day practitioners of recycling are preponderantly relatively conventional citizens, not striving for major changes in the social status quo. In the case of Chicago's recycling, initially scattered individuals were motivated by civic virtue to recycle and to seek public action to protect a common-pool resource, even if established political institutions did not act for a decade. The particular frustration is that laws existed to enhance recycling, but the government refused to implement them; on the other hand, it did not retract them either.

Everyday-Makers and Citizen Elites

The recycling example points to the political participation of "everyday-makers," a term coined by Danish sociologist Henrik Bang (2003). Everyday-makers are people who only occasionally act in politics, mostly in relationship to issues close at hand. Although aware of "big issues," they do not normally participate in regard to them. They are my neighbors who did not demonstrate against the war in Iraq but attended meetings to protest the school board's construction of a wrought iron fence around a school playground to discourage public use of the facility. Everyday-makers are not apathetic to all politics, although they might show up that way on some surveys. They are more active on definite matters impinging on everyday life. Such citizens act to make everyday life better for themselves and sometimes act in a local and specific manner for the commonweal, thereby exhibiting civic virtue as regards some matter.

Everyday-makers are not active in organized political groups and do not attend political events, except sporadically; sometimes they do attend events regarding local, particular issues such as constructing a wrought iron fence around a playground. Everyday-makers can, however, get active on broader issues, even if this is not ordinarily the case. Such involvement happens with environmental pollution in one's own area, a specific, tangible, neighborhood irritant. Opposition to neighborhood pollution leads to specific tangible actions—signing a petition, going to a face-to-face neighborhood meeting. In turn such neighborhood activity can lead to the specific, tangible action of writing a check to a national environmental lobby. The everyday-maker can proceed from specific, immediate action, either out of civic virtue (recycling) or self-interest (getting rid of immediately tangible pollution), to a more general action, such as contributing to a lobby for a public-interest cause. The movement from neighborhood-specific activity to backing a national lobby is a dimension of enhanced political participation.

Everyday-makers can act out of seemingly abstract motives in the area of policy implementation. In his classic formulation, Murray Edelman (1964) described the logic of symbols and political quiescence. Political elites may pass legislation in order to quiet some demand for reform, but such legislation merely symbolizes a concern and has no tangible or specific effects upon public policy if the law is poorly written and unenforceable or if the precipitating issue gets much less public attention. In some areas, however, everyday-makers appreciate the tangible difficulties that ensue if a law is not enforced. In the case of environmental pollution, for instance, tangible evidence of inattention to the law can be very disturbing, leading the everyday-maker to take political action, both to remove the material irritant and to express concern about the need for fairness in government.

Innovative civic participation involves the relationship between leaders and everyday-makers. In the area of environmental issues, the interaction of citizen activists and everyday-makers is central. Activists are the antithesis of everyday-makers; they are politically active almost all the time and may even work full-time as lobbyists, organizers, or elected public officials. As they are connected within networks of those active in some issue, they are knowledgeable about political alignments and technical interpretations of some public issue. In American politics, civic innovation has produced national environmental lobbies managed by leaders who are articulate, well educated, politically knowledgeable, and aggressive. Environmental leadership manages organizations that often have resources amounting to tens of millions of dollars, as the title Christopher Bosso's leading book about the topic, *Environment, Inc.* (2005), reflects.

Polls have shown support for environmental issues is much greater than is suggested by the actions (even the minimal action of sending a check) of those who do anything to support national environmental groups (Shaiko 1999, 29–43). Most checkbook contributors are likely to be politically active; at least this was the case with the government reform lobby, Common Cause (McFarland 1984, 45, 57). But activist managers of environmental groups have an incentive to get inactive everyday-makers to send money. If slightly involved in an organization, some everyday-makers might express opinions to activist managers through occasional blog entries or other Internet communications. Theda Skocpol (2004) has criticized Washington-based public-interest lobbies as managed by technologically sophisticated managerial elites, leaving no room for participation by the everyday-makers sending in checks. On the other hand, such public-interest activists do provide a vehicle for everyday-makers to act minimally in an effective, if limited, way. Here, however, I can only mention, not solve, the puzzle of the relationship between citizen activists and everyday-makers.

Conclusion

Reference to the city of Chicago brings to mind political corruption and its relationship to civic virtue and public action to make and enforce laws for the common good. As Rasma Karklins (2005) has aptly summarized the situation, political corruption means that someone turns the public into the private. The corrupt official either literally or metaphorically sells a segment of the public sphere to a private party, who then owns the public segment (controls government policy for his or her own benefit at the expense of the commonweal). Perhaps contrary to expectation, this Chicago example shows that inadequate policy implementation is not always due to corruption, at least according to some direct definition. Mayor Daley wanted to demonstrate that his preferred mode of public policy was superior to that of those advocating for property owners to sort their recyclables. His administration wanted to keep down public expenditures, although of course unnecessary jobs had been created for political supporters. In addition, the Daley administration did not want to alienate building managers and condo boards, individuals who might be influential within neighborhood social networks.

As the next chapter discusses further, we can speak of "hard" and "soft" corruption. Hard corruption would include illegal activity, such as taking a bribe to rewrite an administrative regulation. Soft corruption in the United States would encompass the acts of a subgovernmental coalition (popularly known as an "iron triangle") in controlling an area of policy for its own interests, especially when that interest contradicts the original intention of legislators. Often the actions of the civic participators in the environmental area actually strengthen the state. This is because in numerous instances, environmental participators are pressing to get the state to enforce the law in the way it was written rather than not implementing it at all, thereby in effect repealing it without public consent. One sees this in the recycling example. Creative participation then often works directly to strengthen the state, which separates this mode of participation from participation in social movements.

Clearly, environmental participation is a very general area for political action, one that is attaining ever greater, global importance. Environmental participation overlaps with other categories of creative participation, not only in its opposition to corruption but sometimes in political consumerism (as in boycotting polluters) as well as in action through transnational advocacy networks. Subsequent chapters treat these types of action.

Environmental participation must be creative political participation because it is particularly subject to the logic of collective action and the tragedy of the commons. Environmental participation is also very largely concerned with the politics of implementation, as governments may pass environmental laws as symbolic support for the commonweal but then neglect to implement them effectively due to economic expense, special-interest pressure, and shifts in public attention. Environmental participation, however, has its appeals for a number of citizens who normally eschew political participation.

CHAPTER 3

❧

COMBATING POLITICAL CORRUPTION

Political corruption is universal: it occurs in all forms of political system, whether democratic or authoritarian; it occurs at all times and in all places. All men are not angels, as James Madison and Andrew Hamilton reminded us. Normally, though, at least a few people will engage in political participation to remedy corruption. Therefore, such participation is also a universal, occurring in different types of political systems and at all times and places. Combating corruption is thus a central aspect of participation as civic innovation. In such situations, scattered individuals, imbued with a sense of civic virtue, seek to remedy corrupt practices but lack established institutions for doing so—probably because the established political institutions are corrupt and thus are themselves the problem to be remedied. Citizens seeking the commonweal must then create strategies of political action and new political institutions to combat the corruption of public institutions.

In my view, the entire Western tradition of scholarship has failed to deal well with the issue of political corruption. Or perhaps one might argue that political philosophy and legal scholarship have much to say about political corruption but recent social science has not adequately presented such knowledge (but see Rose-Ackerman 1999). In any event, I can do only a small bit to rectify this scholarly omission. In this chapter, I follow Rasma Karklins's leading work *The System Made Me Do It: Corruption in Post-Communist Societies* (2005). A student of Eastern European and comparative politics, Karklins found shocking the emerging problem of political corruption in East Europe and Russia after 1989, having been unprepared by academic scholarship for the observation that political corruption is a major obstacle to transitions to democracy. Her resultant book does much to illuminate this universal political problem, and I follow her definition of corruption and use of collective-action paradoxes in analyzing this issue.

The study of American politics has treated the issue of political corruption with a certain sheepishness; it is certainly not a first priority for scholarly examination. American political reformers acquired an elitist image as representing the interests of upper-middle-class white suburbanites, the atypically educated Protestant residents of Belmont, Stamford, Evanston, or Berkeley. Robert Merton and other social scientists urged the empirical study of the functions of the urban political machine, whose patronage politics assimilated immigrants, represented working-class, urban interests, and expressed the political ethos of immigrant Irish Catholics. Criticism of corruption in patronage politics seemed both "unempirical" and ethnically intolerant (Merton 1957).[1]

The question of cultural relativism of corruption must be noted. I prefer not to substitute a functionalist neologism for "corruption." Obviously the term implies a negative evaluation; yet, the interlocutor can easily find contradictions. For instance, almost all readers would have positive thoughts about a Nazi official accepting a bribe to allow a Jew to emigrate. On the other hand, there seems to be an international acceptance of closely proximate concepts of corruption. Observers evaluate corruption in independent countries and publish quantitative rankings. Before, during, and after the tenure of Paul Wolfowitz, the World Bank has sought to describe, evaluate, and combat corruption as an important means to promote economic development (Marquette 2003).

As noted above, I follow Karklins's definition of political corruption as "the misuse of public power for private gain." She writes, "When talking about corruption, people often think only of bribery, but it exists in many other forms" (Karklins 2005, 25); she then appends a page-long list of different types. There are three categories: "everyday interaction between officials and citizens," "interaction within public institutions," and "influence over political institutions." For instance, interactions between officials and citizens include bribery, be it initiated by a citizen or official or organized extortion by groups of officials. Officials may overregulate to solicit bribes or enhance their power. Officials may misuse licensing and inspection powers for personal gain or special political goals.

Under the second category of interaction within public institutions, Karklins lists the self-serving use of public funds, such as hidden salaries, overspending on luxury items, and appropriating cars, apartments, and dachas. A second category includes profiteering from public resources, such as selling off public assets, using public employees for private work, and leasing public property for private gain. A third category encompasses profiteering from privatization and public procurement, such as steering business to oneself, disregarding conflicts of interest and competitive bidding, and taking kickbacks. A fourth category contains influence peddling and manipulation of personnel decisions, such as engaging in nepotism, extorting favors from subordinates or job candidates, and sabotaging personnel reforms that infringe on one's turf.

Karklins third general category is "influence over political institutions." The first item on the list is "state capture," that is, de facto takeover of state institutions, for instance, by building personal fiefdoms or "exploiting public institutions for enrichment of self and network" (economists call this "rent seeking"). Another item is "misuse of legislative power," such as selling laws to private interests, blocking anticorruption legislation, and deliberately passing vague legislation that cannot be implemented. Under this category, Karklins also places undermining elections, corruption of the judicial process, "forming secret power networks to engage in corrupt acts," misuse of investigatory powers, official use of political blackmail, and corruption of the media (all quotes in this paragraph from Karklins 2005, 25).

Speaking from the standpoint of American political culture, I would then speak of "hard" and "soft" corruption. Hard corruption in American politics would refer to the first two categories, generally involving bribery, outright theft, appropriation of government property, violation of personnel codes, and so forth. Such hard corruption is specifically illegal. Following Karklins's general view of corruption as appropriating the public for private use, however, one can refer to soft corruption in the United States. Soft corruption is normally legal, but it is corruption nonetheless in the sense that it deflects public policies for private gain. It is legal and normal political practice to organize coalitions of interest groups, legislative committee members, and subunits of government into subgovernments in a particular public-policy area (popularly termed "iron triangles") to appropriate public policy for private gain, for instance, for a single industry, professional association, business corporation, or limited locality.

Soft corruption is particularly involved in the politics of implementation. Referring to the logic of collective action, ordinarily in American public-policy processes a legislative coalition initiating policy change will weaken over time as coalition partners move on to different political issues, while mass public-opinion believes legislation has settled the issue. Yet, of course, issues are seldom so settled. A small group of corporate, professional, or local stakeholders hostile to the legislation may very well remain organized as the general-public coalition for change dissipates. Having a few, highly motivated stakeholders, the coalition will press for policy change in the implementation process. In the American system, the particular interest coalition will press for administrative and regulatory funding cutbacks, regulatory amendments and exceptions, appointment of administrators hostile to the intent of the original law, delegation of regulatory interpretation to local administrators opposed to the intent of the law, and so forth. This ordinary part of American political processes is normally quite legal and includes practices engaged in at one time or another by almost all active political people. Nevertheless, such implementation politics often involves working for the disintegration of a stated public goal for the benefit of some particular interest coalition. As such, it constitutes soft corruption in my terminology (Lowi 1979).

Thus, one avenue of civic-innovative participation is standing up against the logic of collective action in implementation politics. Such citizens can be said to have civic virtue, to be scattered or diffused interests in Mancur Olson Jr.'s terminology, and to aim to restore the commonweal or public goods in Olson's terminology; they may also very well lack established political institutions to act to restore the original public policy. This is important because implementation politics can be viewed in a general sense as a universal characteristic of politics in general. The role of implementation politics in the American system is readily apprehended, if usually ignored as offensive to the general culture of legality and government legitimacy. But implementation politics factor into all political systems, in every time and place. A perusal of the serious press indicates that this is a fundamental issue for the current Chinese authoritarian system, for example. Thus, how can Beijing get local administrators to cooperate in regulating the local economy for central environmental goals?

This chapter describes three differing examples of political corruption and civic action to combat corruption: one in 1890s Wisconsin, another in contemporary rural China, and a third in contemporary post-Communist systems. My goal is straightforward—I seek to exemplify creative participation as civic innovation and to demonstrate that it is a basic form of political participation. I do not aim to build a casebook for correcting hard and soft political corruption. Actually, a growing and somewhat technical literature deals with how to combat political corruption in the contemporary political world (Heidenheimer and Johnston 2002). The reader may notice how, somewhat paradoxically, creative participation as civic innovation sometimes bolsters the stability of the state by protecting the public against private acquisition.

Wisconsin Political Reform, 1893 to 1900

A centerpiece of the discussion of political corruption in American political history traces the rise and evolution of the so-called Progressive movement for political reform, often dated from 1901 to 1917. Leading Progressives included Presidents Theodore Roosevelt and Woodrow Wilson, as well as Wisconsin governor and senator Robert La Follette. La Follette and his political faction in Wisconsin are remembered as innovators within the Progressive reform tradition, for instance, for their support for primary elections in party nominations and firm regulation of railroad rates, central to transportation at that time. In *The New Citizenship: Origins of Progressivism in Wisconsin, 1885–1900* (1972), historian David Thelen focuses on the question of which pre-1900 political events in Wisconsin shaped the emergence of La Follette progressivism after 1900.

Although Thelen cautiously states that Wisconsin might have been exceptional within the Progressive movement, his study leaves the overall impression that a "new citizenship" formed the basis of Progressive reform. Other theories have emphasized social conflict, such as ethnic, status, and economic divisions between upper-middle-class, white Protestant suburbanites opposing working-class, Catholic (largely Irish) city politicians, the chieftains of the patronage political machine (Hofstadter 1955; Link 1954; Mowry 1958; Hays 1964; Weinstein 1968). Robert Wiebe's (1967) theory of progressivism, though less oriented toward social conflict, stressed the assumption of power and influence by emerging groups of middle-class professionals in a time of burgeoning industrialization and modernization. Leftist scholars interpreted progressivism as a means of masking emerging control by national business elites (Weinstein 1968). Thelen, on the other hand, characterizes progressivism as originating as a communitywide movement against corrupt business-government dominance, bringing together representatives of all economic classes and major economic groups. Thelen takes seriously the statements of local opponents to alliances of local utility rate setters and utility managers that they advocated "the" public interest against the special interests. Public-interest coalitions could simultaneously include both wealthy owners of businesses consuming electricity, subject to rent-seeking rate increases, as well as working-class German immigrants.[2]

Thelen describes a reform process at the city level from 1893 to 1900 as setting the stage for a statewide, organized Progressive politics after that time. In 1893, a severe economic depression disrupted the political and social status quo. Unemployment figures illustrate the severity of the depression:

> At Milwaukee, with 38,850 wage earners in 1890, estimates of unemployment ... [by] a police census ... [were] 11,200 unemployed males in December of 1893.... Most observers estimated that 35 to 40 per cent of the city's workers were unemployed during 1893–1894. Charities officials ... knew exactly how many people had applied for relief. In the prosperous times between 1887 and 1892 the Milwaukee County poor list ranged between 447 and 886 families; in January of 1894 that list numbered 3,430 families.... Two hundred miles away, at La Crosse, a "conservative" estimated that more than half of that city's 3,844 workers were unemployed in the winter of 1893–1894; the story was the same at Beloit and Superior.... A good guess would probably be that the state's unemployment rate fluctuated between 20 and 30 percent during the five-year depression. (Thelen 1972, 58–59)

In other words, unemployment during the 1893 depression in Wisconsin was a bit greater than the national average during the Great Depression years of 1930 to 1935.

One effect of the depression in Wisconsin was the cementing of the special-interest-capture phenomenon, whereby local utilities and local governments supported one another at the expense of the commonweal. At this time local governments within limits set by the state regulated the rates of the previously expanding electric light, trolley, telephone, and municipal water industries. The sudden depression threatened the profits of the locally regulated utilities, whose executives, experienced in influencing local governments, then set about pressuring city councils to increase their rates, cut their taxes, and repeal health, safety, and construction regulations that might endanger profits. Both hard and soft corruption ensued, as the utilities can be said to have controlled the policies of some city governments. Furthermore, as regards policy implementation, utilities sometimes ignored regulations and even direct court orders (Thelen 1972, 280). "By the summer of 1894 Milwaukee officials felt themselves 'powerless' to regulate the street railway company. Sheboygan's three-year failure to regulate the Wisconsin Telephone Company raised 'the vital question' of whether a city 'has the control of its own streets, or whether any corporation can use them as it sees fit.' Ashlanders wondered whether 'the streets of a city are public highways' or whether they belonged to the railroads" (Thelen 1972, 248). Moreover, the utilities frequently managed to get the city councils to lower their taxes, thereby shifting the burden to citizens frequently unable to pay their taxes, resulting in major cutbacks in public services such as police, schools, and roads.

This was a setting for participation as civic innovation. Established political institutions were corrupt, controlled by the utility interests.

> Voters were furious; they could not translate into policy their desire to restore service, fares, or taxes to pre-panic levels if ... [the utilities] opposed them. To counter the parliamentary skills, political organization, and money the establishment commanded, they developed the techniques of mass politics. They learned that their instruments of exposure, mass meetings, petitions, and publicity could defeat the establishment only if voters could directly express their wishes by such changes in political institutions as home rule, secret nominations, anti-lobby laws, and an end to free passes [on rail and trolley systems]. They were trying to change the traditions and operations of city politics. (Thelen 1972, 288)

Thelen then states emphatically, "The distinguishing social feature of the new mass, progressive politics was its unification of men from all classes as consumers, taxpayers, and citizens.... The separate class and ethnic bases that had underlain Milwaukee politics since the Civil War fused under the unifying pressures of corporate offenses" (Thelen 1972, 288). This was participation as civic innovation in that scattered citizens seeking common goods sought new means of public action to combat political corruption.

The citizenry's reaction to the authoritarian rule (elections did not work) of the cliques of paid-off local officials and utility companies was initially active but rather formless. Thelen speaks of mass meetings, petitions, media expressions (local newspapers), and generally unsuccessful attempts at influencing local elections and lobbying the state legislature. Civic innovation was exemplified by the organization of discussion groups after the onset of the depression to discuss the crisis and means of public action to deal with it. "Milwaukeeans groped for answers at the Liberal Club, the Social Science Club, the Ethical Society, the Academy of Social Science, the Church and Labor Social Union, the Economic League, the Social Economics Club, the College Endowment Association, the People's Institute, the Christian Labor Union, and the Forum Club, all but one of which formed after the panic" (Thelen 1972, 70–71). Similar discussion circles rapidly spread through preexisting associations, such as both Protestant and Catholic churches, numerous women's groups, and labor unions. The University of Wisconsin formed extension centers to meet widespread demand to learn the views of its economists.

One mode of public action was the formation of municipal leagues to bring together a communitywide coalition to end corruption. While led by upper-middle-class citizens, municipal leagues sought to represent the different ethnic and economic strata of a community. An organization that at the time received national attention, the Milwaukee Municipal League, was a research group and lobby to further anticorruption reforms such as nonpartisan elections, civil service laws, and the granting of tax exemptions to businesses in return for political contributions or outright bribery. The Milwaukee league became possibly the most successful such civic action league in American urban history. "By the influence of its members, the importance of its city in the state's life, the relevance of its proposals to the needs of cities in a depressed economy, and the energy and brilliance of its state-wide campaigns, the league had overcome some of the seemingly impossible obstacles that stood in the way of state-wide reform" (Thelen 1972, 174).

The anticorruption action eventually achieved a large measure of success.

> The war against the corporations had produced municipal ownership of various utilities, rate regulation on the local level; consumer-owned utilities, prohibitions on free passes for aldermen and legislators, requirements for financial statements by utilities, registration of corporate lobbyists, and enforcement of health and safety requirements. The taxation crusade had forced some wealthy individuals and corporations to pay their delinquent taxes ... raised taxes significantly on the remaining quasi-public corporations [utilities] and insurance companies ... and passed a state inheritance tax. (Thelen 1972, 307)

The anticorruption movement's political success was exemplified by "the increasingly competent, conscientious, and responsive local officials who campaigned against corporate privilege and tax exemptions" (Thelen 1972, 307–308).

I have included this successful protest movement as an example of innovative civic participation. It aimed to enhance the common good, to achieve the public interest in opposition to the control by special interests. Most citizens would find lower utility and tax bills in their personal material interest, but public action to improve the economic lot of the entire community is a commonweal goal. Citizens who attended meetings, engaged in discussions, wrote letters to the editor, canvassed their neighbors, and voted to represent public interests were engaged in civic-innovative participation. This is especially true as such citizens at first could not act effectively through the normal channels of political institutions.

In this case, civic innovation is linked to the other forms of participation. In the numerous discussions of the social crisis alluded to by Thelen, citizens of the entire community were not present, but such discussions entailed consideration of how the entire community might act to oppose political corruption, thereby partially resembling the forum model of participation. The civic innovators captured face-to-face groups of civic engagement, such as religious, women's, and labor groups. The local movements resembled social-movement participation, although most contemporary scholars consider social movements as oppositional to the norms of a social order rather than as attempting to maintain legal norms against corruption (Melucci 1996). Political participation in legitimate American political institutions turned out to be effective because after about four years of organizing, political-party outsider factions began to support the new civic consciousness and to win elections with such citizen support. The outsider faction in the Republican Party was led by Robert La Follette, who after 1900 became Wisconsin's dominant political leader for twenty-five years (Unger 2000).

The reform supporters, in their opposition to political corruption, had the quality of everyday-makers. As Thelen concludes,

> The progressive issues were rooted ... in local problems that threatened everyone. Because the trauma of the depression was local and immediate—the closing of local factories, loss of jobs by friends and neighbors, strikes at nearby plants, death-dealing impure water, increased streetcar fares, higher local taxes, criminal local bankers, fatal accidents at unguarded railway crossings, and declining income for everyone—the reaction was local and immediate. Instead of looking toward national ethnic, professional, or partisan organizations, which were not oriented toward such crises, Wisconsinites worked with their fellow townspeople of all backgrounds ... to control arrogant local individuals and corporations. (1972, 310)

I would conjecture that after the reform efforts succeeded, many of the everyday-makers dropped out of politics and, while they voted in general elections, did not vote in primaries and stopped attending discussion groups and mass political meetings. Nevertheless, the citizens' movements for the public interest, scattered through the cities and towns of Wisconsin in the 1890s, remain an especially interesting case of political participation in American politics.

The Great Depression of 1929 to 1938 apparently did not elicit, to a great extent, behavior similar to the anticorruption movement in Wisconsin from 1893 to 1900. During the twentieth-century depression, those angered by government inaction became active in voting and campaigning for the national New Deal Democratic Party, which was responsive to the concerns of the everyday citizen. More radically inclined citizens participated in a variety of social movements, for instance, by supporting Huey Long, Father Charles Coughlin, the Bonus Army march, international communism, and the guaranteed income movement (Townsendites). The thrust of Democratic Party activism moved toward presidential and congressional elections, rather than aiming chiefly to gain control of local government. Political movements oriented toward the local level did occur, especially before the inauguration of the New Deal presidency, but these local movements were revolts by poor people acting from self-interest rather than public actions by citizens motivated by civic consciousness (Piven and Cloward 1977).

From 1968 to 1975 there was a great upsurge in the organization of Washington lobbying organizations for environmentalism and to protest political corruption (Common Cause). Participation in such public-interest Washington lobbies normally constitutes writing a yearly check, but this is a form of creative political participation, and it is significant as such lobbies have had significant influence upon policy making, representing diffused interests and thereby countermanding the logic of collective action (Berry 1999; Bosso 2005; McFarland 1984). However, such checkbook participation is obviously different from that demonstrated at the local level during the Wisconsin anticorruption movement. Still, after 1980 with the increase of free market, pro-business, Republican Party power in Washington, public action for environmental causes became more operative at the local level, where prospects for success seemed greater (Bosso 2005, 127–143). No doubt several thousand instances exist of such local action for immediate environmental goals; consider again, for instance, the case of recycling in Chicago. On the other hand, I have seen no evidence that local action aimed at local political corruption is a frequent form of innovative civic participation, although such local action does occur through established political institutions routinely. As in Wisconsin, everyday-makers drop in and out of political participation via donating financially to environmental and anticorruption groups, recycling, and participating reactively to local and immediate environmental threats.

Contemporary Rural China

Among the most tremendous social changes in world history are occurring in contemporary rural China. Roughly 700,000 villages, averaging about 1,000 members each, are, for the most part, undergoing modernization, although the rural population is declining due to emigration to urban areas, largely in the coastal areas of China. The political corruption associated with this massive social change produces a great deal of political protest from rural subjects striving to protect ideas of the common good as well as individual self-interest. I follow the tendency in scholarship to discuss changes in rural villages separately from the fundamental changes occurring in Chinese cities.

The Chinese political system is authoritarian and centrally directed. The Beijing government issues directives concerning economic development and industrialization, construction of infrastructure, population control, election of village committees, public health, and, recently, environmental regulations. The directives flow downward through the provincial level, to the county/city level, to the township level, to the village level. The task of implementing policy directives in 700,000 villages, many of them still premodern in economy and communications, is indeed awesome. Widespread hard and soft corruption at the village level is to be expected, if only because of human nature. Beijing in 1987 began establishing elected village committees, but one must expect thousands of instances in which local cliques of government officials and party heads form alliances to undermine and control such elections. One must expect thousands of instances of corrupt local officials controlling land-use policy and taking bribes from entrepreneurs desiring lands for projects, while displacing peasants and ignoring codified rights for land use and repayment for government seizure of land. Following the Soviet idiom, we might call such local corrupt cliques "family circles," since the American terminology of "iron triangles," or subgovernments, is inappropriate (Berliner 1957, 259–263; Ripley and Franklin 1984).

The 1987 issuing of a directive to hold elections for village committees was a historical marker for the central government's willingness to consider sometimes the complaints of aggrieved villagers, whose "claims do not always fall on deaf ears ... because some members of the elite believe that offering redress may help placate the discontented and reduce the likelihood of unrest while improving policy implementation and cadre oversight" (O'Brien and Li 2006, 15). Rural villagers complaining about local family circles are engaged in political participation as "civic" innovation, although "civic" is placed in quotation marks since the overall authoritarian framework does not allow for action based on citizenship as we define it in the West. Rural villagers' protests against local corruption in China can be regarded as a striving to restore public policy as a public good, against officials taking bribes or engaging in arbitrary action to continue in power.

"Discontented villagers increasingly cite laws, regulations, and other authoritative communications when challenging all sorts of cadre malfeasance, including
misconduct related to economic appropriation, grass-roots elections, village
finances, land use, cadre corruption and the use of excessive force" (O'Brien
and Li 2006, 6). Kevin O'Brien and Lianjiang Li (2006) refer to such protest as
"rightful resistance," meaning the villagers cite policies and codes directed from
Beijing against local corruption (not "rights" in the sense of universal human
rights). In this section, I describe Chinese rightful resistance or civic innovation.
I do not imply that this will bring about democracy of citizenship in the Western
sense. Indeed, it seems to me to promote the overall stability of an authoritarian
system. Yet, such political participation is a major form of public action by 700
million people (12 percent of all humans), and from a worldwide perspective, it
must be considered an important form of political participation.

Even according to the official reports of the Beijing regime, there are numerous
protests in rural villages. A Central Committee report on popular protests noted
that "more than 70 percent of 'collective incidents' (*quintixing shijian*) in rural
Shandong during 2000 arose due to 'cadre-mass contradictions and conflicts of
material interests,' and that many of these incidents centered on village elections.
The main points of conflict reported ... [included] elected cadres who were corrupt, overbearing, or unwilling to open village finances; election manipulation;
attempts by lineages or criminal gangs to undermine elections" (O'Brien and Li
2006, 53). Again, the point is that unlike in the Tiananmen Square tragedy, the
rural protests are against not the nature of the national regime but local corruption, as contrasted with policies of Beijing. According to central government figures, such protests are quite numerous, although the following data also includes
urban protests: "Official statistics show that more than 3 million rural and urban
residents took part in 58,000 collective incidents in 2003, a 14 percent increase
over 2002, while the number of protesters increased nearly 7 percent.... In 2004
the minister of public security reported that the number of collective incidents
jumped again, to 74,000, involving 3.76 million people, a dramatic increase from
the 10,000 incidents reported in 1994" (O'Brien and Li 2006, 53).

Increasingly the collective incidents have protested the conduct of village
elections by incumbent village officials, after the introduction of such elections
under Deng Xiaoping in 1987, and a strengthening of the center's local election policy under Jiang Zemin in 1998. Everywhere in the world, local decision
making involves land use, even for zoning and building decisions in the United
States, and corrupt land-use decisions by village family circles have been a general

cause of local protests. Land-use decisions are related to the construction of roads and other infrastructure or of new economic facilities such as industrial plants. Bribery is common in influencing Chinese local governments' land-use decisions. Recently journalists have managed to observe local environmental protests against contamination by industrial facilities, often allowed by corrupt officials to engage in dangerous polluting practices (O'Brien and Li 2006).

To give a picture of rural protest activities, we cite descriptions of such protests given in O'Brien and Li's *Rightful Resistance in Rural China*. These authors use a three-point scale of protest: first, publicizing corrupt policies; second, demanding dialogue or discussion with the aberrant officials; third, direct confrontation (O'Brien and Li 2006, 69–70). Of course, publicizing an issue and bringing more people to one's side is a basic political strategy, as discussed in E. E. Schattschneider's *The Semisovereign People* (1960) and in the major works about agenda setting by Bryan Jones and Frank Baumgartner, such as *The Politics of Attention* (2005).

The least confrontational of O'Brien and Li's classifications of direct action in contemporary rural China

> might be called publicizing a policy. In the course of "studying" (*xue*) or "disseminating documents" (*xuanchuan wenjian*), activists make known or distribute materials that (they contend) show that county, township, or village cadres have violated a central or provincial directive. They do so for the purpose of alerting the public to official misconduct and mobilizing opposition to unapproved "local policies" (*tu zhengce*). The documents they select always relate to issues that concern villagers greatly, be it reducing excessive taxes and fees, decrying the use of violence, or promoting well-run village elections.... Activists have publicized the following materials: President Jiang Zemin's 1998 speech on reducing "peasant burdens" (*nongmin fudan*) ... and the 1993 Agricultural Law ... especially its clauses ... that forbid imposing unlawful fees, affirm the right of villagers to "reject" (*jujue*) unsanctioned exactions, and stipulate that higher levels should work to halt such impositions and have them returned to villagers. (2006, 69–70)

One example of such protest occurred in Hengyang county of the Hunan province, when, according to the O'Brien and Li interviews, one man "rented some audio equipment, set it up on his roof, and aired central and provincial documents about easing peasant burdens to his entire village" (2006, 70). O'Brien and Li cite an example of an effective protest:

According to several Hengyang protest organizers, on market days they sometimes simply set up a loudspeaker in the town center and read out documents concerning tax and fee reductions that were issued by the center, Hunan province, or Hengyang city.... Township cadres, when they heard the Hengyang activists disclosing fee limits on a busy market day in 1998, first cut off electricity to their loudspeaker. But a sympathetic restaurant owner stepped in and supplied the villagers with a generator. Then, a number of officials came out of their offices and ordered the protesters to disperse, only to find themselves upbraided for impeding the lawful dissemination of central policies. (2006, 71)

In a different province, Henan, interviews revealed similar protests involving the mass study of government documents, when activists organized "'ten thousand-person meetings' (*wan ren dahui*) in a government compound to study policies that excoriate corruption or limit fees.... Activists in Xinyang county, Henan, for example, have organized numerous mass meetings (the largest of which township officials estimated drew more than 6,000 participants) to publicize central policies and provincial regulations" (O'Brien and Li 2006, 72).

The Chinese call a more confrontational mode of protest than publicizing government anticorruption policies

"demanding a dialogue" (*yaoqiu duihua*).... Activists and their supporters, often after collective petitioning or publicizing a policy fails to budge their foes, may insist on face-to-face meetings with local officials (or their proxies) to urge immediate revocation of unlawful local measures. Rightful resisters have used this tactic in Hengyang most notably to fight mounting school fees. Because many townships can no longer collect as much revenue as they used to (owing to both pressure from above and resistance from below), and many poorer districts are financially starved in the wake of the 1994 fiscal reforms, township leaders have frequently allowed local schoolmasters to increase educational fees on their own. Self-styled "burden-reduction representatives" (*jianfu daibiao*), usually after hard-pressed parents come to them for help, may demand that all overcharges be returned. Instead of lodging a collective complaint, which would have been more common in the past, a group of representatives may proceed directly to the school. The arrival of these "peasant heroes" (*nongmin yingxiong*) typically attracts a large crowd, not least because the parents who invited them often encourage onlookers to come. (O'Brien and Li 2006, 73–74)

The most confrontational mode of protest is direct confrontation. To illustrate, we cite another example from the O'Brien and Li interviews:

In early September 1996 three activists arranged a movie presentation [to gather a crowd] to read out a Hunan provincial document that reduced peasant burdens.... A skirmish broke out with township officials.... Two days later, more than six hundred villagers, carrying banners and flags, beating drums and gongs, and setting off fireworks, paraded down the busiest street in the township to the main office building to insist on a meeting with the Party secretary and the government head. (2006, 74–75)

Another example of face-to-face defiance occurred in 1998 "in Hengyang county. Two 'burden-reduction representatives' had locked horns with township revenue collectors when they tried to prevent the collection of several unauthorized fees. When the officials struck one of the representatives with a flashlight, a shoving match broke out. Again, angry villagers responded, this time overturning two jeeps the township cadres used for their work" (O'Brien and Li 2006, 75).

O'Brien and Li describe a direct confrontation occurring in the local election process when

a group of villagers in Hubei [province] successfully disrupted a villagers' committee election in which nominations were not handled according to approved procedures. Just as the ballots were being distributed, one villager leapt to the platform where the election committee was presiding, grabbed a microphone and shouted: "Xiong Dachao is a corrupt cadre. Don't vote for him!" Immediately several of his confederates stood up and started shouting words of support.... The assembled protesters then tore up their own ballots, as well as those of other villagers who were milling about waiting to vote. (2006, 75)

Such creative participation to enforce laws and regulations by means of loudspeakers, contentious public dialogues, and public confrontation illustrates the problems of a half-formed legal system and a partially disintegrated state system. Of course, Beijing is aware of this, hence maintains as a high priority developing legal Chinese Communist institutions so that directives from the center can be implemented adequately, rather than undermined by corrupt village officials.

Meanwhile villagers engaged in such creative participation do sometimes get their way. Their main political resource is the threat of disruption; local cadres may lose their jobs even if demonstrations are forcefully eliminated. Together, hundreds of thousands of such demonstrations over a decade could disrupt the stability of the Communist regime. Since such anticorruption participation is normally based on laws and regulations directed from the center, and since the threat of disruption is serious, higher authorities sometimes side with village protesters and remove offending local officials or otherwise intervene to redress the protested wrongs. Consequently, the outcome of the thousands of protests may be to lessen the degree of local corruption and actually help stabilize the regime by gaining support from villagers and successfully implementing central directives.

If a protest exceeds a short sequence of demonstrations, dialogues, and confrontations, the burden-reduction representatives lobby higher levels of authority beyond the village (township, county, province, center) and engage in bureaucratic politics. In other words, within the large and heterogeneous hierarchies of party and state, the civic strategy is to find one of the many agencies or party officials who might support the burden reducers' cause, perhaps as part of some ongoing competitive process with rival agencies or political cliques. Post Deng Xiaoping, newspapers are less closely directed, so autonomous journalists will sometimes publicize village corruption, all in the name of supporting the state.

Of course, protesting villagers do not always win. No one has been keeping score. O'Brien and Li leave the impression that the Chinese civic activists sometimes win but usually lose (2006, 11–15, 80–81). Even though the rightful resisters allege violation of governing laws and regulations, township and county party and government officials are likely to have political alliances with local officials, or to be partially responsible for the infractions of corruptions, or to feel threatened by social disorder and the possible organization of new, contentious local power cliques. A sort of intermediate outcome exists. Authorities frequently yield to most of the grievances advanced by protestors, while arresting one or more of the leaders of the protest (O'Brien and Li 2006, 87). This would be like administrators at the University of California, Berkeley, in 1964 supporting the arrest of student leader Mario Savio, while admitting to using student card tables on campus to recruit political supporters.

In some instances, participants in village "collective incidents" are primarily motivated by material self-interest, such as protecting land ownership. However, descriptions of the incidents imply a widespread desire to alleviate civic injustice, as in the case of activist burden-reduction representatives, who themselves are investing personal time and the risk of arrest or beatings by police. This is a Chinese version of political participation in which the participants contradict the logic of collective action by supporting a cause for the good of the entire village community. As protesters against local corruption and defenders of the legal order, the Chinese participants in rural activism are the cousins of the Progressive protestors against corrupt utility deals in 1890s Wisconsin.

The tens of thousands of collective incidents per year occur independently of one another, arising in scattered, separate villages to protest immediate, local corruption. Many of the participants in such civic action are likely to be everyday-makers, supporting efforts to correct palpable, immediate local infringements of legality by corrupt, local officials. Such everyday-makers watch the protest succeed or fail, then do little in the way of civic participation for the next several years. Everyday-makers are not inclined to frequent political participation in support of abstract, national goals. On the other hand, evidence suggests that some civic activists stay in the game, form networks within a local county, and are recognized as leaders by their peasant colleagues (O'Brien and Li 2006, 102–112). We may speculate as to the consequences of activist "burden-reduction representatives" in 100,000 villages communicating through the Internet. This would constitute an innovative form of opposition that might carry over from opposition to local corruption to support for more general, abstract advocacy of national legal change. Still, such a large network of burden reducers is unlikely to emerge, as the central government maintains a workshop of expert Internet hackers to disrupt the formation of networks countering the political regime (Chase and Mulvenon 2002).

From the standpoint of sheer enumeration, Chinese rural rightful resistance is a major form of creative participation as civic innovation. While the term "civic" does not carry the same meaning as in the context of Western citizenship, this form of political participation acknowledges the need for public action to maintain the public good against political corruption. Rightful resistance is also public action to maintain legality in cases in which the established political institutions are unable to act. Perhaps somewhat paradoxically, the rural protests may achieve some success and thereby act to maintain the established authoritarian state.

Focused Participation: Post-Communist Societies

Since 1989 analytical observers have viewed the emergent post-Communist societies of Eastern Europe and formerly Soviet Asia as politically corrupt. However, scholars and journalists have not chronicled local public action against local public officials, as occurred in Wisconsin and rural China. There can be a certain degree of alliance formation among national civil-society organizations, including participation of the worldwide nongovernmental organization Transparency International, to fight political corruption, as Karklins found in Latvia (Karklins

2005, 140–142). It seems that the significant forms of political participation as civic innovation take place in post-Communist societies as a result of the influence of focusing events and places, occurring in national-level politics.

Focused participation is defined in terms of the logic of collective action. The costs of collective action for the individual participant are lowered if everyone expects everyone else to gather at a particular place at a particular time. In my own experience as a student and faculty member at the University of California, Berkeley, from 1962 to 1974, all political activists and observers of campus events knew that on any given day, those interested in politics would gather at Sproul Plaza in front of the administration building at noon. During times of heightened political tension, activist organizers knew that thousands of people would show up at this time and place, reducing the costs of organizing public action. On the other hand, in the days before the Internet, protest-inclined students needed to expend little effort to determine where to go and when to express their opinions and act. Participants also expected many others to show up because circumstances focused organization at a particular time and place, and because all expected a large turnout, everyone's expectation of successful public action increased. Of course, Olson's logic would still apply. Some students might elect to become free riders and eschew taking a five-minute walk to Sproul Plaza. My assumption, on the other hand, is that people motivated by civic virtue will not become free riders, especially when the costs of participation are especially low.

Political scientist Joshua A. Tucker has applied the idea of focused participation to the so-called color revolutions in post-Communist societies. Tucker argues that corrupt elections in these societies served as a participation focus in a manner analogous to "Sproul Plaza at noon" in Berkeley. In Serbia, Ukraine, Georgia, and Kyrgyzstan, color revolutions ensued after incumbent governments, widely viewed as corrupt, held national elections with outcomes determined by political corruption. In these four countries, mass demonstrations in the capital city held shortly after a controversial election overthrew the corrupt incumbents. The elections were national, held and affecting everyone at the same time. After calls by opposition parties to demonstrate against the corrupt outcome, everyone came to see a high probability that tens or hundreds of thousands of others would turn out at the same time to demonstrate against a violation of civic justice. Perhaps some would hold off joining the demonstration for the first day or two, but seeing tens of thousands in the streets apparently making headway for the cause, the laggard participants would then join. In the instances of the color revolutions, there was also a focusing place, the streets of the capital, especially any central plaza close to major government buildings (Tucker 2007).

The archetypal color revolution was the Orange Revolution in the Ukraine in 2004 to protest the outcome of a national presidential election "marked by widespread instances of voter fraud—including the illegal expulsion of opposition representatives from election commissions, multiple voting by busloads of people, absentee ballot abuse … as well as dramatic changes in turnout figures [in the government's strongholds]" (Tucker 2007, 538). Massive demonstrations and a long-term campout in the central squares of Kiev ensued. A year earlier, during Georgia's Rose Revolution, 100,000 people congregated in the capital, Tblisi, to protest the suspect outcome of national legislative elections. In 2005 in Kyrgyzstan, according to the head of an election observer mission, a national election was "undermined by vote buying, registration of candidates, interference with media and worryingly low confidence in judicial and electoral institutions on the part of voters and candidates" (Tucker 2007, 538). Subsequently, 30,000 protesters converged in the main square of Bishkek, the capital, and offending president Askar Akayev fled the country. Earlier, while not graced with a color appellation, similar events occurred in 2000 in Serbia when manipulative and authoritarian president Slobodan Milosevic declared himself winner in a reelection, while the aggregate of 25,000 poll watchers from the opposition stated otherwise. Shortly thereafter, 200,000 demonstrated in the capital, Belgrade, and after the Serbian Constitutional Court annulled the election, 500,000 turned out in support of the decision, leading to Milosevic's resignation (Tucker 2007, 537).

Opposition parties called for protests in the Ukraine, Georgia, and Serbia, but many participants were likely motivated by civic virtue, that is, the desire for public action to oppose political corruption for the common good, rather than sheer political factionalism. Interviews with 468 participants in a similar protest against corrupt elections in Serbia in December 1996 provide evidence for this. When given a multiple choice of reasons for joining the protest, with more than one answer allowed, 59.6 percent referred to "desires for justice and free elections," 23.8 percent referred to "overthrow of communism," 23.2 percent referred to "construction of a new society similar to those in Western Europe," 17.8 percent referred to "overthrow of personal rule of Slobodan Milosevic," and only 3.9 percent referred to "support of opposition leaders" (Lazic 1999, 63).

While the four color revolutions discussed here all succeeded in driving out an incumbent leader, subsequent events proved disappointing to many protestors, and in fact the Ukraine's new leader, Victor Yushchenko, Georgia's Mikhail

Saakashvili, and Kyrgyzstan's Kurmabek Bakiyev have all been accused of political corruption (Tucker 2007, 542). Further, if focusing times and places make civic action easier to organize, repressive authorities may also understand the role of focused participation. For instance, authorities can seek to manipulate elections by means other than dramatic fraud on election day: They can control the media, harass the opposition during the nomination process, and find excuses to declare oppositional candidacies illegal, as has been done in contemporary Iran. Authorities can seek to block travel to the focusing locations, such as by eliminating train and bus service to the capital. Therefore, we can expect focused participation and color revolutions to succeed only occasionally in instituting democratic governments.

Nevertheless, focused participation is a means of correcting the logic of collective action. It reduces the costs of scattered individuals in getting together for public action for the common good. Focused participation helps in combating *political* corruption when existing institutions are useless or need bolstering in their opposition. It enhances political participation as civic innovation.

Conclusion

Political corruption is common in various types of political systems and at various times, although there is cultural variation in identifying its forms. One type of creative participation to combat corruption might be called the Madisonian strategy: Madison advocated adopting a new constitution, partly because a higher level of government could diminish majority tyranny at the lower levels. As in the Chinese rural protests, creative participation against corruption sometimes means expanding the span of conflict to bring in higher- or central-level government power to combat the power of lower-level, corrupt political cliques. In such cases, creative participation against corruption means organizing a very wide sector of the local community against the narrow constituency of the corrupt local power clique. A parallel type of creative participation is when protestors act at the local level of the national capital to protest electoral corruption by the overall national government.

Anticorruption participation is not closely tied to political consumerism (see Chapter 4) or transnational advocacy networks, except through limited participation in Transparency International (see Chapter 6). However, political corruption in the twenty-first century often involves deals among local officials to disobey central pollution regulations to increase the profit level of local factories or to enable local political leaders to construct public works projects. This problem occurs in many different political systems. Creative participation then ties together environmental protest (Chapter 2) and anticorruption protest.

Notes

1. Rehearsing the sins of political corruption can get old in short order; of course this or that public official is going to steal money, take bribes for contracts, or hire incompetent employees. Calling for reform and studying the lives and actions of reformers can also reach a dead end as I discovered after ten years' research (1974 to 1984) into Common Cause (McFarland 1984).

2. Statements about "the" public interest must be viewed in the context of Olson's logic of collective action. Actually, in most public-policy situations, there may be several public interests. The question is how they are represented. Progressive reformers were actually stating that oligopolistic rate manipulation was defeating the public's interest in economical utility rates as the general public was not represented in the rate-setting process. However, there might be another public interest in a situation, such as providing sufficient capital for the utilities to construct improved service facilities.

CHAPTER 4

❧

POLITICAL CONSUMERISM

Attending the national meeting of the American Political Science Association in 2001, I was a bit dumfounded to see a paper titled "Shopping As Political Participation" listed in the official program. Actually, the paper was being delivered not to an official association panel, but to an associated group, meeting in conjunction with the national association of political scientists. Shopping as politics? What was that? No red-blooded guy would do research on such a topic! A female colleague of mine then teaching at the University of Stockholm was presenting the paper (Micheletti 2001).

Nonetheless, the phrase "shopping as politics" stuck in my mind. Did I not myself, once a week, make a consumer choice, based more on political than economic criteria? Did we not accept without question similar phenomena to the politics of shopping as topics for political science? Although the term did not come into general use until the 1890s, we accept the boycott as an important political and social-movement tactic. After all, the boycott of tea, textiles, and other London-taxed British imports was an important organizational and identity-forming precursor to the American Revolution. Mahatma Gandhi's boycott and substitution movement for imported British textiles similarly became a major organizational and identity-forming strategy in India's independence movement. American political scientists are familiar with the use of the boycott as a strategy in the African American civil rights movement, although particular boycotts were generally contained to targeted local merchants and institutions within a particular geographical area. Accounts of the Montgomery bus boycott and the actions of Rosa Parks now form part of an all-American political folklore. Those concerned with the theory of American social movements, labor organizing, and the situation of Latinos in America have studied the famous boycott of California table grapes by Cesar Chavez and the United Farm Workers (Jenkins 1985). Political boycotts to organize consumer shopping decisions are an established topic for study by social scientists and historians (Friedman 1999).

But what of cases of politicized shopping that are not so closely tied to social movements? In 1937 to 1940, many young American women refused to buy silk stockings to protest the Japanese invasion of China (Glickman 2005). Around 1980, hundreds of thousands of women (perhaps more than a million) around the world refused to buy Nestlé products because the Swiss conglomerate promoted the use of its baby formula in the Third World, which sometimes resulted in polluted water being substituted for breast milk (Sethi 1994; Micheletti 2003, 59–61). In the late 1990s, many college undergraduates in the United States refused to buy Nike sneakers, then at the height of youth fashion, due to the alleged sweatshop conditions under which they were manufactured in East Asia (Bennett 2004). In 2000, supporters of Focus on the Family and the American Family Association, as well as dedicated southern Baptists, refused to buy Disney products due to alleged homosexual favoritism, although, despite the large membership of these collectivities, very few actually participated in this boycott (or likely discontinued watching ESPN and refusing to rent Disney videos) (*New York Times* 2005; Cosgrove-Mather 2005). In 2009, I would estimate that more than a million households avoided shopping at Walmart, reflecting a preference against the company's antiunion policies or its homogenization of local shopping environments. In line with a massive public shift toward supporting environmental action around 2006, mercantile establishments, both great and small and including Walmart and Home Depot, began to advertise green merchandising practices in order to attract shoppers who use the political criterion of greenness to override strictly economic considerations. Might all of this be called "political consumerism"? Is this a form of political participation? If so, does this not confirm the view of Pippa Norris (2002b) that the problem of civic engagement is not as great as it at first seems?

Departing from boycotts organized by social movements or from shopping actions encouraged by committees that are perhaps of a quasimovement nature, political shopping is an everyday action for many individuals, who are simply expressing their political views through shopping decisions. Pulling into a Shell station to get a needed refill, our driver explained to me and the two other passengers, "I'm sorry that I'm not going to Citgo, but I have to get gas right now." (Citgo had offered to subsidize the fuel expenditures of poor people living in the Bronx.) Had there been a Citgo station across the street, we would have pulled in there, even if the price per gallon were ten cents higher. But, of course, economics is still part of political consumer decisions, and if the price per gallon were twenty cents higher at Citgo, we would have reluctantly patronized Shell, unaware of the particulars of the boycott against Shell for its conduct in the Nigerian delta.

Granted that for most people economic criteria are usually the most important in shopping decisions, we might conjecture that two million individuals in the United States make one political shopping decision almost every day. This would constitute 730 million political acts per year by this group—a most impressive number in terms of quantity of political participation. In terms of exercising political influence, that is, changing the course of political events, the effect might be quite limited. In any case, political science does not have much to say about such political participation—or even about whether it is "political."

Social science concern for political consumerism, as described above, does exist in Europe. One strain of thought originated with Danish political scientists and was picked up by Swedish political scientist Michele Micheletti and German political scientist Dietlind Stolle. These two (especially Micheletti) put political consumerism on the map of European social science between 2003 and 2005 (Instituttet for Fremtidsforsning and Elsam 1996; Micheletti 2003; Micheletti, Follesdal, and Stolle 2004). In particular, they influenced Jan van Deth, holder of a political science chair at Germany's Mannheim University, to include items about political consumerism in a large-scale survey of twenty-two European countries (van Deth 2010, ch. 5).

Van Deth's Citizenship, Involvement, Democracy (CID) survey is representative of social and political involvement. The CID project applied "a very broad conception of 'involvement,'" including "modes of participation which go beyond the traditional concepts of both 'conventional' institutionalized modes of participation and 'unconventional,' non-institutionalized, protest activities. In particular, the concepts of 'political consumerism' and of 'small democracy are covered'" (van Deth 2008, 12). The CID survey is based on a general question that is subsequently applied to nineteen modes of participation, plus "other activities": "There are different ways of attempting to bring about improvements or counteract deterioration in society. During the last twelve months, have you done any of the following?" (van Deth 2008, 12). Van Deth comments about the general question: "In this way, no references are made to politics or government in conventional terms, but to the much broader concept of activities aimed at 'improvements or [to] counteract deterioration in society'" (van Deth 2008, 12). Thus, two of the nineteen activities indicated in the survey are "boycott certain products" and "buy certain products." The percentages of those giving positive responses to these questions are indicated in Table 5.1 of the next chapter. Germany, Russia, and Spain are included in the survey, but the United Kingdom, France, and Italy are not (van Deth 2008, 30–31).

At this point I simply want to note that there are enough political consumers in Europe to make the concept important in the study of political participation. One outstanding finding is that three Scandinavian countries, Denmark, Norway, and Sweden, have high levels of political consumerism, corroborating the image of Scandinavian political culture as public oriented. In a 2005 survey of political involvement in the United States, 18 percent of Americans responded that "during the last 12 months" they had "boycotted certain products," while 22 percent responded that "during the last 12 months" they had "deliberately bought certain products for political, ethical, or environmental reasons" (see the U.S. "Citizenship, Involvement, Democracy" survey at www.uscidsurvey.org).

Economists have done little research into political consumerism. However, a few policy-oriented economists have begun to study what they term "green consumption," that is, consumer behavior in which environmental preferences override standard economic preferences. A paper by economists Clifford S. Russell, Signe Krarup, and Christopher Clark (2005) excellently summarizes early research by economists about green consumption. (Significantly this paper was written for a conference in Denmark, not the United States.) The authors note that "there is accumulating evidence that green consumption can, and in fact does, occur," and they cite "reported instances in which substantial increases in firm market share have closely followed the awarding of a positive environmental label to a particular product" (Russell, Krarup, and Clark 2005, 8). This is evidence from actual behavior as reported by the U.S. Environmental Protection Agency. Surveys measure attitudes or self-described behavior, but still Russell, Krarup, and Clark report that "respondents to surveys, oblivious to the dictates of economic theory, generally indicate that they are concerned about the environment and quite willing to purchase, or have in the recent past purchased, green products" (2005, 8).

Here the three authors cite the work of six different research teams. "In addition, there have been many studies asking consumers, in a variety of different ways, whether they are willing to base consumption decisions at least partly on the environmental attributes of goods and services" (Russell, Krarup, and Clark 2005, 8). But they caution the reader, "Of course there is a vast difference between a hypothetical response to a survey and a costly action, and, not surprisingly, there are studies suggesting a divergence between the expressed desire to purchase green products and actual purchases" (Russell, Krarup, and Clark 2005, 8). Here the authors note that there is evidence that consumers have actually been influenced in specific empirical situations by eco-labels denoting preferred green consumption as regards seafood, electricity purchasing, detergents, and paper towels. Russell, Krarup, and Clark state that "the very existence of green products and the accompanying 'green advertising' imply that companies (or at least their marketing departments) believe that consumers are willing to consider environmental issues when making purchase decisions" (2005, 9). They mention that there "is anecdotal evidence of companies whose sales dropped precipitously as a result of being labeled environmentally unfriendly" (Russell, Krarup, and Clark 2005, 8–9).

In conclusion, evidence is mounting that a significant number of consumers make purchasing decisions sometimes based on political preferences. This is true in Europe, the United States, and especially in Scandinavia. Here, we need to continue with some discussion of whether and when such political consumerism is actually political and how we may initially conceptually map political consumerism as participation in the political process.

Political Consumerism: Environmentalism and Branding

A good way to approach the study of political consumerism is to focus first on shopping decisions reflecting a preference for improving the environment. Such consumerism can be considered a form of political participation in the sense we have discussed already. Of course, we can say that sometimes consumers put an economic value on improving the environment when they purchase a product. But we can also say that, at the same time, they are projecting a political opinion, especially if they spend more for a green product. By making a purchase following green criteria, a consumer thus subordinates a personal, material interest to a concern for the realization of a common good.

In addition, I wish to focus on political consumerism as a form of creative political participation in its civic-innovative dimension. This was a useful aspect of Micheletti's (2003) reframing of the discussion of consumerism away from an initial consideration of altruistic economic decision making or as a subject in the history of social movements, such as Indian independence, the struggles of labor in the United States and elsewhere, and the black civil rights movement. As a first take on the phenomenon, political scientists can emphasize the political-participation and policy-process aspects of the political consumerism. This perspective makes it possible to ask questions in surveys about whether a person has purchased or boycotted a product in the last year with a view toward social betterment or prevention of social deterioration.

Rather than initially blocking the flow of thought with a discussion of "what is political?"—a question going back to Aristotle—let us consider political consumerism as a political process, with its individual participation, formation of groups, influence attempts, and feedback interactions from government. With a concern for civic innovation, we can look to political consumerism at work within the process of environmental policy making in the United States and elsewhere.

A central concern in political consumerism is the politics of corporate branding. The modern economic idea of the brand occurred with the processes of product marketing in the nineteenth century. With rail transportation, it became increasingly possible to manufacture consumer goods in large quantities in concentrated locations. However, it also became necessary to communicate images of quality by out-of-town manufacturers to compete with those better known in the local environment. Thus, product symbols were created and most importantly expressed in product labeling. The goal was to associate the product symbols with the idea of good product quality.

In the twenty-first century, global producers aggregately spend billions in advertising directed toward enhancing a brand's reputation through marketing. If the brand's name and advertised symbols have a favorable reputation among millions of people, sales and profits are protected and enhanced (Vogel 2005, 52–53). Of special interest is the refinement of the brand into a logo or symbol familiar to tens of millions: the McDonald's arches, the Coca-Cola script, the Microsoft wavy diamond, the Nike swoosh.

Consequently, political consumers' relation to branding and brand names is important—especially as out-and-out purchasing boycotts of consumer products seldom work on a national basis, as it is difficult for corporate decision makers to identify sales losses directly resulting from a boycott, if such losses do indeed exist. (The situation is different in the case of localized boycotts, such as those common during the black civil rights movement.) However, a corporate decision maker may preside over a brand name worth hundreds of millions or even billions—value that is, for example, monetized in corporate mergers. It is of extreme importance for corporate leaders to protect and enhance their brand name's reputation. Hence, an efficient strategy used by political consumers seeking to change corporate policy is to threaten the good reputation of the corporate brand. Actual reduction in sales through a consumer boycott is secondary in effectiveness.

This focus on the politics of a corporate brand is recognized in the literature of the politics of business, the politics of shopping, and the writing of influential activist leader Naomi Klein (2000). In the last half of 2006, manufacturers and retailers of U.S. consumer products began a major new emphasis on their products' environmental quality, as well as their companies' environmentally friendly practices, such as reduced energy use. Active agitation by environmental groups and consumers must have contributed to this change in corporate branding policy, although such changes must be viewed as part of a process of political consumerism, masking identifiable cause-and-effect relationships. Some of the factors involved in the process of political consumerism, environmentalism, corporate brands, and political participation can be seen in an attempt to boycott oil behemoth ExxonMobil.

Political Consumerism and ExxonMobil

ExxonMobil is of course the world's largest oil company, formed in 1999 by the merger of two giants, the Exxon and Mobil oil companies. Since the *Exxon Valdez* oil spill off the coast of Alaska in 1989, Exxon has been the target of constant criticism from environmentalists, who were particularly incensed when Exxon appeared to stall in paying court-imposed damages following the disaster. Browsing the Internet reveals that after 1995, at any given time, three or more separate boycotts of Exxon centered on different environmental goals—preventing global warming, blocking attempts to drill for oil in wildlife refuges, conducting research into the development of alternative energy sources (see www.coopamerica.org and www.exxposeexxon.com). As we have seen, political consumerism does exist, and being one of the two largest American corporations in terms of sales figures (with Walmart), ExxonMobil would inevitably be a target of political consumerism unless it organized a superb public-relations campaign to quiet criticism of its policies.

However, ExxonMobil refused to make public statements that contradicted its profit-making policies. Lee Raymond, Exxon's CEO from 1993 to 2005, was perhaps the most prominent corporate CEO to deny evidence of global warming (in 2007 a new CEO claimed that Raymond had been misunderstood) (Krugman 2006; Nocera 2007; Krauss and Mouawad 2007). In 2001, British Petroleum initiated its public-relations statements of concern about global warming and said it would devote research money to developing alternative energy sources (Frey 2002). Shell Oil followed suit (Macalister 2003), and by 2004 a parade of large and small oil companies was lining up to declare concern for global warming (Corporate Social Responsibility Newswire 2004). On the other hand, ExxonMobil and Lee Raymond refused to change the company's position on global warming, research into alternative energy, and its role as a profit-making corporation. In fact, in 2006 Exxon made $39.5 billion in profit, apparently then an all-time record for a private corporation (Nocera 2007). From 1998 to 2005, Exxon gave about $2 million per year to various researchers, who might be expected to issue reports indicating that the evidence for global warming was uncertain (Adam 2006).

By 2005 the brand name ExxonMobil was widely associated with a corporation opposed to environmental protection, certainly among environmentalists in a position to influence the brand's image among politicians and journalists. Internet communications regularly referred to ExxonMobil as distinctively worse on environmental issues than any of the other American or European oil giants (the Russians and the Chinese were not part of this picture). Exxon increasingly became a target of political consumerism, not only as one of the two largest corporations but as one with a distinctively antienvironmental posture.

Since the onset of widespread public participation on the Internet in around 1994, thousands of people have posted statements criticizing ExxonMobil's policies every year. Frequently, such anti-Exxon postings call for a boycott of Exxon and Mobil gasoline (different geographical areas feature one or the other brand). The Internet regularly shows new postings among anti-Exxon individuals discussing the best strategy for a boycott, in light of the observation that Exxon is making huge profits and a drop in sales at a few hundred gas stations will make little difference to its managers. Consumers generally recognize the impracticality of an idea circulated continuously since 1999: If an individual called a boycott and circulated the boycott message to thirty friends by e-mail, and if each of the thirty friends then circulated the boycott message to thirty of their friends, and so forth, a massive boycott could be rapidly generated. Most Internet users remember that such invitations to action were common in the 1990s, but the e-mail chains were speedily broken. Another discussed strategy was to form a committee and call for a boycott of Exxon gas stations on only one day a week, when gas station trade would noticeably drop, thereby indicating to management the possibility of a more widespread, threatening boycott.

Of course, in recent years consumers have suffered a steep, albeit fluctuating, increase in gasoline prices. Many consumers believe that the gas-price increase is mostly due to manipulation by ExxonMobil and other large oil companies, adding to individuals' motivation to boycott Exxon—although I would describe this as a self-interested rather than a civic motivation to prevent global warming. Of course, following Mancur Olson Jr.'s logic of collective action, spending time and money to boycott on the basis of a price increase requires some participatory motivation to override material self-interest. Anti-Exxon individuals would probably sign up eventually for one of the boycotts previously organized by a group.

In July 2005, a coalition of environmental lobbies launched a major boycott known as "Exxpose Exxon" (www.exxposeexxon.com) directed against the company's policies concerning global warming, refusal to invest in renewable energy, support for drilling in the Arctic wildlife refuge, and delinquent payment of punitive damages from the *Exxon Valdez* oil spill. A political campaign (including a boycott) was launched by Defenders of Wildlife, Greenpeace, Natural Resources Defense Council, the Sierra Club, U.S. Public Interest Research Group, and the Union of Concerned Scientists—five leading environmental groups and an organization of politically concerned scientists. The anti-Exxon campaign had the support of twelve other groups, including, to name a few, Environmental Action, Friends of the Earth, National Environmental Trust, MoveOn.org Political Action, Public Citizen (the Nader group), and True Majority (founded by Ben Cohen of Ben and Jerry's). These groups are all "checkbook groups" in terms of membership, although a small number of Sierra Club members do have face-to-face meetings. MoveOn, the well-known Internet group founded to protest President Bill Clinton's impeachment, has since evolved into a major campaign fund-raiser and petition organizer for liberal causes. The eighteen public-interest lobbies organized a headquarters for the boycott with a substantial Internet presence. Exxpose Exxon got significant traditional press at the time of its launch in 2005 (Barringer 2005). Word of the boycott spread via the communications networks of the eighteen constituent organizations.

The anti-Exxon campaign managed to put significant pressure on Exxon management, although a decrease in gasoline purchases cannot be tracked and was likely insignificant in relation to Exxon's overall sales. The group claimed 500,000 supporters, although political groups usually exaggerate such numbers (www.exxposeeaxxon.com/highlights.html).

In August 2007, Exxpose Exxon did claim the following, which gives some evidence of its activities: 50 rallies in 50 cities at gas stations; a rally of 150 at a national shareholder's meeting; 2,300 people calling Exxon headquarters on an anniversary of the *Exxon Valdez* oil spill, while the next year 23,000 faxes and 400 mailed letters were sent urging payment of damages due to the spill. The group also claimed that supporters had met with 200 Exxon or Mobil gas station managers, urging them to protest the corporate management's environmental policies. Fifty people were organized to show the critical film *Out of Balance: ExxonMobil's Impact on Climate Change.*

Regarding Congress, the group claimed 1 million e-mails sent protested Exxon policies, and 60,000 letters sent protested the Department of Energy's request that Lee Raymond head a National Petroleum Council advisory study of America's energy future (National Petroleum Council 2007). Further, it said it had influenced Senators Olympia Snowe and Jay Rockefeller and House Science and Technology Investigations and Oversight Subcommittee chairman Brad Miller to send two letters to Exxon protesting its funding of global-warming denial studies. Exxpose Exxon also sent a delegation to the UN Climate Change Conference in Canada to distribute flyers and press materials.

Regarding media, the campaign cited 16,000 visits per month to its website, the issuance of four critical research reports about Exxon's global-warming policies and the group's lobbying on energy issues, as well as its coverage by major newspapers, the Associated Press and Reuters, and major TV and radio networks. Exxpose Exxon had created a one-minute Flash animation (for Internet viewing) critical of Exxon that was seen by 50,000 people. In addition the group claimed that 2,000 letters generally critical of Exxon had been sent to newspapers, as had 2,700 letters critical of Exxon's global-warming policy and 800 letters critical of the selection of Lee Raymond as head of an energy study commission (see www .exxposeexxon.com/highlights.html and www.exxposeexxon.com/action).

As is frequent in the analysis of political consumerist campaigns, it is difficult to isolate whether the campaign itself changed the action trajectory of the corporation. Lee Raymond retired as ExxonMobil CEO in December 2005, after heading the company since 1993. His successor, Rex W. Tillerson, gave a widely publicized speech in February 2007 accepting the idea that carbon dioxide emissions cause global warming (Krauss and Mouawad 2007), which was interpreted as indicating a policy change by ExxonMobil to a position of greater concern about the issue. About a year after the Exxpose Exxon campaign began, the company announced cutbacks in its funding to various groups performing contract research denying global warming. Exxon would not give specifics, but Greenpeace posted research indicating a cutback of $1.4 million in funding to various denial groups. This would be a 40 percent cutback according to Greenpeace, although I would estimate a greater percentage because some of the Exxon money apparently promoted conservative causes other than denying global warming (Greenpeace 2007). Exxon public-relations statements in 2007 emphasized that the company was "widely misunderstood," that it had been concerned about global warming while firmly arguing that capital should not be wasted on premature regulation of carbon dioxide emissions and firmly arguing that fossil fuels would remain economically central for at least a generation (Krauss and Mouawad 2007; MSNBC 2007).

In any case, it seems that ExxonMobil had changed its position on global warming and would devote less time and money to obstructing new public policy to deal with the issue. It is not possible to determine whether the Exxpose Exxon campaign had much to do with this change; corporate executives would never admit that it had as doing so would only encourage future consumerist campaigns. On the other hand, political consumerists could interpret the rather sudden and significant change in ExxonMobil policy as a victory. In any case, the amount of Internet posting about Exxpose Exxon apparently declined after the summer of 2007.

The ExxonMobil example illustrates that political consumerism must be understood as a process of interaction among individuals, groups such as public-interest groups, and business. Though also part of the process, government did not figure in this brief example. The political-consumerism process may be transnational, as the next chapter discusses. Within this process, political consumerism is political participation as civic innovation in those cases when the goal is the achievement of some common good. Since the mid-1990s political consumerism has normally been based on participation coordinated via the Internet.

Significant instances of political consumerism are likely to feature efforts to change the policies of powerful corporations. The major strategy used against corporate power is the threat to undermine the popularity of its brand. A worldwide business is unlikely to be fazed by a boycott by 500,000 consumers in terms of its immediate profit expectations. However, a powerful corporation will likely be concerned about media publicity that tarnishes its brand and public image, which is necessary for long-run profitability. Furthermore, corporations rely on having an unsullied brand to influence Congress and local governments to win legal support to protect its profits or enable it to expand, for instance, to get permits for the construction of new manufacturing facilities. The ExxonMobil brand, to a considerable extent, communicated lack of concern for environmental deterioration, weakening its requests for earmarked tax reductions, drilling rights, permits for construction of refineries, and so forth.

In the ExxonMobil example, criticism of the oil company brand became part of the political struggle to frame the significance of the global-warming issue as an imminent problem versus one not requiring government action. Control of the political agenda is a source of political power, and successfully framing an issue to get it on the decision-making agenda is a successful exercise of power. In the political-consumerism process, criticism of the corporate brand may lead a corporation to modify its stance in framing a political issue for public decision making.

The Consumption of Water

A political universal is public participation to lessen the pollution of drinking water. In addition, there is often a need for public participation and coordination to preserve and divide limited water supplies. The consumption of water is another area in which consumer interests overlap with environmental interests. In such situations, the implementation of public water policies in many different types of political systems will sometimes go awry. In less developed nations, the public water supply may be contaminated by human and animal wastes. In more developed economies, factories sometimes discharge pollutant chemicals into public water supplies. Generally speaking, a central government, whether democratic or authoritarian, will enact policies to provide safe water unless it is very lacking in administrative capacity. But all governments have problems with policy implementation. We can expect that in many places and at many times, local special-interest cliques will violate clean-water laws when it is costly to prevent pollution. The agricultural or industrial producer will sometimes be protected by local authorities, who seek to protect the profitability of the local industry or have simply been bribed or otherwise influenced by favors from the producing interests. As such it is also a political commonplace for the consumers of polluted water to ascertain the extent of the pollution and to protest the actions of polluters and local special-interest cliques. Protests against failure to implement clean-water policies or to apportion legally limited water supplies are often characterized by creative participation as civic innovation, at least to the point of getting established political institutions involved.

Action to get clean water sometimes has an anticorruption dimension, in addition to its consumer and environmental facets. In rural China, scholars find the most common protests to be against corrupt land deals and electoral fraud (Li and O'Brien 1999). But contemporary China is experiencing vast environmental problems related to massive industrialization processes, some of which involve polluting public water supplies. The jailing of controversial environmental activist Wu Lihong, who made a career of protesting the pollution of Lake Tai, China's third-largest lake, received worldwide attention. Afterward, the central government attempted to enforce its antipollution policies more effectively by issuing new regulations, but it remains to be seen how well the new regulations will be enforced against local cliques seeking to maximize economic development (Bradsher 2008; Kahn 2007).

Provincial protests against water pollution in China are reminiscent of local politics in the United States in the 1890s, when privately owned utilities sometimes furnished water to a community. For instance in Ashland, Wisconsin, citizens formed a civic federation in 1895, with a governing committee including "among others, eleven laborers, three of them unskilled, seven small merchants, six clerks and salesmen, three lawyers, three doctors, three women, two manufacturers, two bankers, one railroad superintendent, and one Swedish Lutheran minister"(Thelen 1972, 178). This may have been a triumph of "bridging" civic engagement across social boundaries, as well as a case of civic innovation. The Ashland Water Company had refused to spend money to extend its intake mains further into Lake Superior, even though Ashland had suffered annual typhoid fever outbreaks. By 1895, "Mayor McClintock had virtually conceded his inability to force responsible actions from the company" (Thelen 1972, 181). However, the Ashland civic federation then threatened the water company with political and legal retribution, thereby provoking the company to compromise and extend the intake mains and reduce water rates.

Another sort of civic-innovative participation involves pollution of drinking water and has received attention in Hollywood films. *Erin Brockovich*, for which Julia Roberts won an Academy Award for playing the title character, tells the story of a young legal assistant's role in coordinating a protest effort against water pollution by the giant Pacific Gas and Electric Company. Because, as usual, there was some ambiguity in assessing the degree of danger from the water pollut-ant hexavalent chromium, a lawsuit on behalf of the citizens of the small town of Hinckley, California, was settled in 1996 for $333 million (Foote 2000). A similar case involved alleged pollution of drinking water in Woburn, Mas-sachusetts, by W. R. Grace and Company and Beatrice Foods due to improper disposal of trichloroethylene and perchloroethylene near two city water wells (Woburn Hydrogeology Data). In this case also, an activist lawyer working with a committee of citizens brought lawsuits subsequently settled out of court. This example of creative participation was made famous in the novel *A Civil Action*, made into a movie in 1998 starring John Travolta and Robert Duvall. Millions of people saw these movies, encouraging other examples of civil action by other Erin Brockoviches seeking public participation to maintain public health against a local economic-development clique.

Common-pool resources, Nobel Prize winner Elinor Ostrom's term for the resources subject to the tragedy of the commons, are often contested in civic-innovation politics about water, as we think of "pools" of water. Ostrom's classic *Governing the Commons: The Evolution of Institutions of Collective Ac-tion* developed out of her study of policies regarding water resources in the Los Angeles area. Pumping competitions developed among various industrial and municipal users of water as they sought to take as much as they could before everyone else used it up. Without the development of regulatory institutions, the common-pool resource would be diminished and consumed in an irrational manner. The policy area of water consumption needed its Erin Brockoviches, both among citizens and representatives of local utilities, to act to form a new institution for the common good of all residents in the Los Angeles area. In this case, civic activism consisted not of suing a local special-interest clique but of working cooperatively to create a new government institution to act for the common good.

Environmentalists can use civic action as a general strategy to attain clean water. Few can object to working to attain clean water for public health and safety, especially for small children who usually suffer the most from chemical pollution in water. Members of an advocacy coalition to attain clean water in a given locale might undergo "political learning" (Sabatier and Jenkins-Smith 1993) and become more concerned with other environmental issues, such as the more controversial problems associated with global warming. This strategic point was made to me by an activist for clean water in New England who actually saw global-warming issues as having a higher priority than fighting water pollution, but expected that industry would block action on carbon dioxide issues unless environmentalists converted more supporters to their cause through work on clean-water and other less expensive issues.

Creative participation as civic innovation results from the politics of water-consumption issues in many times and places. Flaws in policy implementation by various types of governments will result in recurring local pollution issues and public participation to eliminate these problems. Throughout the twenty-first century, water-scarcity issues will impinge upon the politics of China and the American Southwest. Civic activity to preserve this common-pool resource will thus become very important.

The Dixie Chicks Boycott

After 2000, the two American consumer boycotts receiving the widest attention have been those against Walmart and the Dixie Chicks, a group that had produced a number-one country music album. While neither boycott has earthshaking significance, both represent political participation. As Walmart boycotts have generally been organized by unions, I would classify them as an offshoot of the politics of established political groups. The boycott of Dixie Chicks radio play, CD purchases, and performances apparently originated as a spontaneous reaction of tens of thousands of country music fans, although the action was later furthered by two country music radio chains, Cumulus Radio and Cox Radio. In my terms, the Dixie Chicks boycott serves as an example of political consumerism, hence, of creative participation. This indicates that not all examples of political consumerism are related to sustainability, transnational political action, or "politically correct" causes. Other types of action for conceptions of the common good do exist.[1]

The Dixie Chicks boycott should be seen as more than an irrational outburst by right-wing devotees of country music. Another common motivation, recurrent in discussions of the boycott, relates to an idea of citizenship and loyalty, namely, that Americans should remain loyal to their country during international crises, and they should show this loyalty by supporting their president. Social scientists were surprised to find that support for President John F. Kennedy reached its highest peak during the Bay of Pigs crisis, an example of foreign policy incompetence. Now generally expected by social scientists, such support for the president during international crises is called "the presidential rally effect." This widespread attitude can be seen as expressing an idea of loyalty and citizenship: When the nation is under international pressure, supporting the nation's leader, the president, is acting for the common good. Loyalty and support for the United States, the country of freedom, has been the basis for a number of hit songs in the country genre since the nation's entry into Vietnam, which has not been the case for other popular music genres. Support for the president in a time of crisis is a specific form of the generalized notion of loyalty.

On March 10, 2003, Natalie Maines, lead singer of the Dixie Chicks, broke the loyalty norm at a performance in London, England. The arrival of hundreds of audience members after a demonstration against U.S. war preparations against Iraq (the invasion happened nine days later) affected the atmosphere at the performance. The Dixie Chicks had a number one country hit, "The Travelin' Soldier," about the sorrow of the girlfriend of a soldier killed in Vietnam, which fell well within the country music norm of loyalty to the military. In the segue to the song, the incautiously outspoken Maines stated to the audience that opposed President George W. Bush, "Just so you know, [we're on the good side with y'all. We do not want this war, this violence, and] we're ashamed that the president of the United States is from Texas." The brackets indicate a passage omitted tens of thousands of times when the statement was subsequently quoted on the Internet and elsewhere (Democracy Now! 2007). Millions of country music fans were also aware that all three Dixie Chicks were lifelong Texans.

Maines's disloyal statement was greeted with a cheer, but no large demonstration occurred subsequently, and the performance continued. The offending statement, eliding the bracketed material, was seemingly quoted in only one media outlet, the *Guardian*, in a review placing the statement toward the middle, framed by an argument that the Chicks were evolving into aggressive feminists. Before the advent of the Internet, Maines's incautious statement would likely have escaped further notice in the United States. But a country music website, CountryNation.com, posted the review with the inflammatory quotation. The performance took place on March 10, the *Guardian* review appeared on March 12, and by the end of the day, a call for a boycott already had appeared on the Internet discussion group rec.music.country.western. On March 13, country music radio stations began receiving calls demanding a boycott of the Chicks; for instance, two stations in Kansas City and one in Nashville reported receiving hundreds of such complaints. The Associated Press then picked up the story, immediately generating wide discussion on the Internet among country music fans. The issue was communicated to conservatives by FreedomHouse.com, an information and discussion clearinghouse for conservatives, and by right-wing bloggers. On March 14, the Associated Press reported that two country music stations were boycotting the Chicks, and a rush began. Shortly thereafter, most country music stations had joined the boycott, their representatives later explaining doing so was necessary to retain audience acceptance.

The boycott had an immediate effect. The Chicks' album fell off the country music charts, although it declined only slowly on the general music chart (the Chicks had crossed over and by this time appealed to a general audience). This reaction predicted the Chicks' future as an economic enterprise. Prior to the boycott they had sold out an American tour, with 600,000 sales. (At an average of $55 per ticket, I estimate this equaled $33 million. If country music CD sales fell by a million at $17 per album, that is $17 million. Thus, the boycott involved substantial sums of money.) The Dixie Chicks boycott lasted in strong form for more than three years. In March 2003, Maines had tried to conciliate the boycotters by, among other things, issuing a public apology to President Bush. But the level of anger on both sides was great, and after receiving death threats, hiring security guards, being trashed obscenely on the Internet, and initially receiving no support from the country music world, Maines and her cohort fought back by satirizing the boycotters in *Entertainment Weekly*, restating their criticism of the president on national television, and selling obscene T-shirts attacking top-ten country artist Toby Keith, who displayed his patriotism by performing against a concocted backdrop of Maines with Saddam Hussein.

In March 2006, three years after the offending incident, the Chicks released a new album, *Taking the Long Way*. Its major single release, "Not Ready to Make Nice," attacked the boycotters and was seldom played on country radio. On the other hand, the release achieved the number one position on the general pop music charts, indicating that the Chicks could still sell more than a million copies of an album—but to the pop music, not the country music, audience. Initially it seemed that the boycott might destroy the Chicks' financial position in country music, but the widespread publicity had led to counterboycott behavior, albeit without much coordination outside of relatively unorganized Internet linkages. In July 2006, the Chicks arranged a promotional tour for their new album, but ticket sales in several southern cities were insufficient to support performances (Leeds 2006); however, ticket sales did well in the Northeast, and according to the Wikipedia account of their "Accidents and Accusations" tour, new performances were scheduled in Canada, where the

Chicks had gained popularity among Canadians who intensely disliked Bush (Wikipedia, "Dixie Chicks").

Taking the Long Way was the sixteenth best-selling album in the United States in 2006; it won the pop music establishment's 2007 Grammys for Best Album and Best Song and in three other categories (Leeds and Manly 2007). Since there is no "boycott" central, one cannot define an official end to the boycott, but the receipt of five Grammys indicated that the Chicks would maintain their successful careers despite the boycott. It is difficult to assess how much money the Chicks actually lost as the boycott led to increased spending for their music by political liberals, Canadians, and perhaps fans in the United Kingdom.

The Dixie Chicks boycott provides an example of political consumerism and creative participation and illustrates that such political participation can be conservative as well as liberal. In my view, the participation initially stemmed from a spontaneous reaction to Internet and newspaper communications. It was very swift—too swift to be part of a planned right-wing campaign. If two radio stations in Kansas City and one in Nashville received about 1,000 complaints on March 13, 2003, one can estimate that the more than 1,000 country music stations received tens of thousands of complaints. However, critics of radio conglomerates argue that owners of country radio station chains were initially behind the movement. As publicized in a hearing of the Senate Commerce Committee in July 2003, Cumulus Media, Inc., owner of about fifty country stations, and Cox Communications, owner of a similar chain, had both ordered their local affiliates not to play the Dixie Chicks. At the hearing, Senator John McCain, the Commerce Committee chair, denounced this centralization of media control, even though he was among the strongest supporters of the cause in Iraq. However, a statistical analysis of radio playlists by a social scientist indicated that the initial rate of drop-off of play of Chicks' songs was no greater in chain stations than in independently owned ones (Rossman 2004). This tends to verify Cumulus CEO Lewis Dickey Jr.'s statement that his decisions to ban the Chicks came only after local affiliates had already decided to do so in response to local complaints. Dickey's excuse failed to mollify McCain, who viewed the corporate ban as an example of media consolidation beyond the bounds of good public policy (Associated Press 2003).

The Dixie Chicks boycott might be seen as an interesting example of a "red versus blue" cultural controversy. But inspection of Internet materials, including blogs, reveals expressions of opinion beyond the common irrational effusions of rage. Common statements implied that Americans should remain loyal to their president, especially in conducting themselves outside U.S. borders. In other words, some country music fans believed the Chicks should be sanctioned for violating a norm of citizenship, implying belief in a mode of civil conduct for the common good. Such political consumers boycotted the Chicks due to their particular interpretation of the role of citizen.

Conclusion

Political consumerism occurs when scattered consumers seek public action for the commonweal but regard established political institutions as of secondary relevance. Instead they choose to act directly against offending corporate producers, many of them giants in the world economy. Some political consumerism is spontaneous, generated with minimal coordination from television or Internet messages. Such spontaneous action will likely be coordinated by established political groups (e.g., unions) or political entrepreneurs if it seems that many members of the public support the issue.

Political consumerism is often expressed in the choice either to buy or not to buy a product. Consumer boycotts have varying effects but seem unlikely to reduce the income of multinational giants like ExxonMobil substantially. Nevertheless, corporations rely on their symbolic logos to communicate with the public. Consequently, symbolic actions critical of a corporate logo can have an effect over the course of a decade or so on corporate decision makers seeking to maintain a positive public image for their logo.

I do not aim here to worship the consumer boycott—only to study it. Boycotts are not always "politically correct," as is demonstrated by the boycott of the Dixie Chicks in support of the American presidency or by tendencies in different times and places for anti-Semites to boycott Jewish merchants.

Water may be the most important item humans consume. As such public action for clean water directed against polluting firms constitutes an area of creative participation in which political consumerism and environmentalism overlap. In the United States, initial public action may be an instance of political consumerism, but such action is then likely to be expressed by litigation within judicial institutions.

Of course, political consumerism and environmental action are not necessarily limited to one country. Hence, it is relevant to explore creative participation in transnational advocacy networks.

Note

1. This and succeeding paragraphs are based on Rossman 2004; Clarke 2003; CNN.com 2003; BBC News 2003; Tyrangiel 2006; Associated Press 2003; Boliek 2003.

CHAPTER 5

POLITICAL CONSUMERISM IN FOUR
POST-COMMUNIST COUNTRIES

AN EXPLORATORY LOOK

Catherine S. Griffiths

Do post-Communist democracies use marketplace consumption as a tool to express political demands and preferences? Over the past thirty years, our world has witnessed drastic transformations in political regimes and economic markets, from the growth of democracy worldwide to the phenomenon of economic globalization. In the transition from communism to democracy following the collapse of the Soviet Union in 1991, the former Communist countries created from the remnants of the Soviet Bloc transitioned from totalitarian governmental systems with little citizen input into young-and-fledgling democracies with new opportunities for citizen engagement for the first time in decades. Eastern Europe's transition to democracy also led to radical economic changes, from markets that were closely state controlled into emerging forms of capitalism and open markets that privatized many businesses and introduced foreign investments. This major transformation of the Soviet region occurred during the heyday of worldwide market globalization, creating an interesting dynamic for markets and consumers all over the planet, especially in these new economies. As the introduction of new goods from around the world provides consumers with more choices than ever, consumers now wield unprecedented power in spending their dollars.

This confluence of forces is providing citizens with new opportunities for political action through increased market-based politics by using their purchasing power to influence politics, not only in older, free market democracies but also in young democracies with emerging markets like those in post-Communist Eastern Europe. Political science and sociology scholars have recently focused attention on this phenomenon of consumption as political behavior. Termed "political consumerism," it is a nontraditional or creative form of political participation that involves individuals using market choices such as purchasing or boycotting products to enact policy changes (Svendsen 1995; Micheletti 2003; Micheletti, Follesdal, and Stolle 2004). Evidence has emerged that such unconventional participation is increasing on a global scale, even in post-Communist Eastern Europe (Andersen and Tobiasen 2001; Norris 2002b; Inglehart 1997). There are questions about the role that political consumerism plays among other forms of participation, as well as concerns that political consumerism could become either an exit strategy for those who are disheartened with politics or a substitute for traditional political behavior among those groups who previously have been excluded and alienated from conventional participation.

This chapter aims to provide a descriptive examination of political consumerism across Europe, specifically in four young post-Communist democracies—Czech Republic, Hungary, Poland, and Slovenia—and to pose questions and suggestions for further research on this phenomenon among young democracies. While these emerging democratic systems are no doubt still imperfect, major political and economic transformations have allowed citizens to engage in ways they previously had not, both at governmental levels through policy making and voting and in the marketplace through expanded consumer power and access to freer markets. In such cases in which the government and market are simultaneously transforming into democratic and liberal entities that arguably respond to both citizens and consumers, citizens may begin to view the market as just as legitimate an arena for politics as democratic institutions of government (e.g., conventional participation). Due to a collective history of negative interaction with conventional participation methods, citizens in such countries may incorporate political consumerism into their normal political participation behavior at a much earlier stage than in other countries. Hence, in post-Communist states political consumerism could become a mainstream tool in the citizen toolbox and develop as a much stronger force in these countries than in established democracies with long histories of policy change through democratic institutions. First, I review political consumerism and theories surrounding consumption as political behavior, including its potential positive and negative consequences for democratic political participation. I then relate the phenomenon of political consumerism to the study of four post-Communist Eastern European countries and provide a statistical overview of political-consumption trends for them, followed by implications and suggestions for continued research in this growing field of interest. Initial findings show that political consumerism does occur in post-Communist countries, although certainly not at levels on par with those in long-standing, open-market democracies. Still, data shows that political consumerism exists among these nations and even reaches surprising levels in certain post-Communist countries. The initial findings provide encouraging signs for continued study of political consumerism in developing democracies and may provide insight into the ways in which political action repertoires change and expand in the age of globalization.

What Is Political Consumerism or Political Consumption?

The concept of political consumerism is defined by Michele Micheletti, Andreas Follesdal, and Dietlind Stolle as "consumer choice of producers and products based on a variety of ethical and political considerations" related to consumers' values and beliefs (2004, xiv). Such political purchasing activities arguably give consumers more power in the political sphere to use their market choices and dollars as a mechanism to enact change. Micheletti, Follesdal, and Stolle point out that the goal of political consumerism is to induce producers, corporations, and governments to "change objectionable institutional or market practices" (2004, xiv). When citizens attempt to create such policy changes through economic activism, the market becomes a tool for political expression and change, thereby making political consumption a legitimate form of political participation. In *Political Virtue and Shopping*, Michele Micheletti argues that the phenomenon of political consumption, a term she defines as the "power relations among people and choices about how resources should be used and allocated globally," stems from "the politics behind products" (2003, x). In this sense, consumers can take political action on issues outside the traditional nation-state sphere by acting as citizens in the marketplace. Political consumption is *political* specifically because it does not conform to the simple rational-choice market perspective of utility maximization, wherein consumers purchase products in order to receive the highest return for the lowest cost with no specific regard for political or ethical issues (Micheletti, Follesdal, and Stolle 2004; Andersen and Tobiasen 2004; Micheletti 2003; Friedman 1980). In other words, getting the most for your money by shopping at Costco or Walmart for "low prices, everyday" should be seen as utility-maximizing behavior in the marketplace and nothing more. On the contrary, boycotting Walmart because it fails to pay a living wage or provide health benefits for its employees is a prime example of political consumption since consumers are protesting objectionable practices in the marketplace in the hopes that companies or the government will take measures to change these practices.

Micheletti (2003) details five of the most common forms of political-consumption behaviors in modern times: (1) *boycotts* (negative political consumerism) in which consumers intentionally refuse to purchase a specific product or brand name, (2) *buycotts* (positive political consumerism) where consumers purposely purchase specific products and brand names, (3) *labeling schemes* providing consumers with information about the politics behind products (e.g., union made, eco-friendly, fair trade), (4) *stewardship certification* where producers and companies agree to abide by certain guidelines established by a third-party monitor, and (5) *socially responsible investing* whereby consumers can invest their financial resources in stocks and funds that support values and beliefs in line with their own. Not surprisingly, the most common types of political consumption are boycotts and buycotts because they are relatively easy for individual consumers to engage in and perhaps better known than other forms of political consumption. Still, all five of the consumption behaviors outlined by Micheletti encompass both individual and collective activity, meaning they can be coordinated by an organized group or simply taken on by individuals who care about certain issues. One important factor is that political-consumption behaviors are most effective when aggregated among collective actors; in reality, they depend on coordinated actions among many individuals to achieve the desired outcome (Pellizzoni 2007; Micheletti, Follesdal, and Stolle 2004; Micheletti 2003). After all, there is strength in numbers, and as with the individual vote in a national election, the impact of one person's purchasing decisions will likely be minimal. Large numbers of people taking collective action to boycott or buycott a specific product or producer will likely not only garner widespread attention but also create a real impact on a producer or government and prompt a change in policy.

Criticisms of Political Consumerism, Factors Affecting It, and Consequences for Democracy

Different disciplines express interest in the phenomenon of political consumption for varying reasons, approaching it from different theoretical perspectives: reflexive modernization (Beck 2000), ecological modernization (Fisher and Freudenburg 2001), and risk society (Beck 1999) in sociology; governance and postmodernism (Inglehart 1997, 2000; Micheletti 2003) in political science. These areas consider the impact of globalization and individualization in modern society on the personal and political behaviors of people worldwide. If globalization is the product of a world not bounded politically or economically by nation-state lines, it has also intensified the effects of such a world. Problems originating in one state more easily cross state boundaries through personal, political, and economic conduits made possible by modernization. Because consumption now transcends barriers between the political, social, and economic spheres, proponents of political consumerism have good reason and opportunity to address what they see as negative government or market practices through intentional conscious consumption in the marketplace.

While it is still an "emerging form" of political action and an emerging field for scholarly research, political consumerism has ignited a debate in the academic community (Micheletti, Follesdal, and Stolle 2004). Scholarship on the phenomenon of consumption as political behavior has increased recently and raised new questions about the consequences of using markets as political tools and how much value to place on consumerism as an effective tool for political action. Political consumerism is one of the new forms of political activity gaining interest among social scientists because it has unique consequences regarding the future of traditional political activity and for its potential effects (positive and negative) on democracy in general. Negative effects might be that political consumerism could become either an exit strategy for those who are disheartened with politics or a substitute for traditional political behavior for those groups who previously have been excluded and alienated from traditional means of participation. Some concerns about political consumption arise out of fear that it could lead to a weakening of traditional political and civic participation by citizens because they may see it as a more effective tool for policy change than traditional avenues like voting or contacting their elected representatives. Or it could simply be an additional action mode incorporated into the political-action repertoires of already-active individuals, alongside voting, party politics, and civil society.

Individuals and groups who have been systematically excluded or alienated from the political process have only had unconventional means through which to participate until their groups were brought into the realm of conventional political actors (Norris 2002b; Micheletti 2003; Micheletti, Follesdal, and Stolle 2004). Over time, and often through employment of unconventional methods of participation discussed above (protests and boycotts), the province of political action in democracies was forced to expand and allow more groups within societies to participate in those traditional forms. Perhaps those who are members of previously excluded groups have a tendency to engage more in unconventional methods, such as political consumerism, and would consciously segregate themselves from conventional political action. If political consumerism is specifically a form of political protest used by marginalized groups and those who are dissatisfied or disillusioned with conventional participation methods, then it would seem unlikely to decrease existing levels of conventional participation among people who are already active politically and not marginalized.

On the other hand, when conventionally active citizens do not see the fruits of their participation labor over long periods, they may eventually believe that the system has failed, leading to low trust in government institutions and causing citizens to abandon conventional methods in favor of unconventional means, like protests and political consumerism (Stolle, Hooghe, and Micheletti 2005). It could be argued that most citizens of post-Communist countries, having a history of low trust in government institutions (Howard 2002), have seen few positive results from the small amount of conventional political participation they were allowed to engage in as citizens under communism and even after. Precisely because political consumerism functions outside the traditional realm of politics, it could easily be a more attractive option for those in post-Communist countries where people have meaningful access to conventional methods and there is widespread distrust in government institutions and actors.

Regardless of the reasons *why* citizens might choose to participate in political consumerism (e.g., they belong to dissatisfied or excluded groups), there are concerns that their doing so could lead to a weakening of traditional political and civic participation. Citizens may see political consumerism as a more effective or less cumbersome tool for policy change than traditional avenues of electing officials or impacting complicated lawmaking processes. Such ideas foment fears in some scholars of a continued decline of social capital, civic engagement, and political activity as a result of increased political consumerism. They claim that over several decades in the United States and other Western democracies, conventional forms of participation have already been declining, from "voting and joining political parties" (Micheletti, Follesdal, and Stolle 2004) to engaging in civil-society organizations and activities (Dalton 2008; Blais et al. 2004; Wattenberg 2002; Fiorina 2002; Norris 1999, 2002b; Dalton and Wattenberg 2000; Putnam 1995, 2000). These concerns are legitimate, but studies by Barnes and Kaase (1979) and Sidney Tarrow (2000) indicate that these fears are unfounded and that those who engage in unconventional methods do so as a supplement to, rather than a substitute for, their existing activity in conventional forms. In the most extreme case, political consumerism could lead to a serious weakening of democratic processes, which could lead to the eventual disintegration of democratic institutions and governance over time. Essentially, the state could fail, leaving a power vacuum susceptible to takeover by corporate governance. Since political consumerism circumvents the institutional policy process and directly targets market structures, corporations may actually usurp power from traditional democratic institutions while bolstering their own power to create policy through market interactions. Feigenbaum, Henig, and Hamnett (1998) and Norris (2002b) discuss the concern that decision-making power could move away from elected representatives through the process of privatization and end up exclusively in the hands of corporate executives. While it seems far-fetched to think older democracies would fall victim to this fate, it is important not to dismiss this concern when thinking about post-Communist young democracies whose newly minted democratic institutions and government structures are not as well embedded or highly functioning as those in older democracies.

On the other hand, a handful of scholars contradict the "decline" theorists' argument, claiming that they fail to see such new forms of activity as legitimate political engagement. For example, young people tend to eschew traditional forms in favor of "participating in looser and less hierarchical informal networks as well as lifestyle-related, sporadic mobilization efforts" (Stolle, Hooghe, and Micheletti 2005; Bennett 1998; Eliasoph 1998). Other studies have shown that women are more likely to engage in nontraditional forms of participation that are outside the state sphere and closer to their own, traditionally feminine shopping sphere (Stolle and Micheletti 2003; Micheletti 2004; Ackelsberg 2003; Burns, Schlozman, and Verba 2001; Bohstedt 1998; Williams 1998; Orleck 1993). In thinking about this in relation to post-Communist countries like Hungary and Poland, it must be recognized that citizens of such countries do not have a strong history of meaningful conventional political engagement since many citizens were systematically excluded from conventional methods during the Communist era.

The lingering psychological affects of political nonparticipation have taken their toll, leaving individuals disillusioned with conventional participation but also fearful of unconventional methods due to harsh punishments enacted by their governments (Howard 2002).

Why Is Political Consumerism Important for Post-Communist Countries? A Research Question

Micheletti (2003) takes the view that political consumerism has become a standard element of political participation repertoires in Western society today, meaning that, while it may not be seen as more effective or important than voting or volunteering, citizens consider it an effective and legitimate expression of their political opinions and goals in certain situations. It seems natural that the phenomenon of political consumption would already have strong roots in long-standing Western democracies in Europe and the Americas, where there is a history of free markets combined with strong democratic institutions. In fact, despite the long-established ties between democracy and free markets, such connections do not guarantee the use of markets as political arenas in all such societies. Still, established and mature democracies with open economies and higher average incomes can be expected to have higher levels of political-consumption activity, in part because they have more disposable income to spend on political purchases and in part because their economies offer greater political opportunity structures through which consumers can make market-based political decisions.

These questions should not, however, be limited only to established, open-market democracies. There is some value in asking these questions about developing democracies that have only recently opened their economies and governments to incorporate citizen-consumer behavior as a norm. Such cases present an opportunity to examine if and how political consumerism becomes integrated into the political and economic structure of a society. Post-Communist countries present unique factors for study in this area. Their newly opening economies, while at different stages of globalization and foreign direct investment, provide an opportunity for citizens to increase their personal economies through wages and give citizen-consumers an opportunity to spend their dollars (or zlotys) in politically conscious ways because they are being provided with more products and producers from which to choose. Yet, one might expect the marginalization concept to emerge in such countries as well. During their time under Soviet rule, most citizens in these countries were either forced to participate in mandatory conventional political actions that were essentially meaningless, or they were systematically marginalized or prohibited from participating in political action at all (Howard 2002). As a result, citizens in post-Communist countries might prefer to use unconventional methods, such as the market, for political action over state institutions because they are simply used to being excluded or because they have little trust in state government to perform its duties. They might essentially confirm Micheletti's findings that those who are marginalized or denied access to established political structures are more likely to use the market than other political modes to express their political opinions.

Other studies consider the possibility that such citizens are more willing to engage in political activity because the opportunity costs of doing so are lower now than they have been since the onset of communism in the early 1900s (Vanhuysse 2004). In the past, citizens were often severely punished for expressing political beliefs that did not fall in line with the ruling party's platform. After communism fell and former Soviet regions gained their independence from the central grip of Communist Party rulers, new "democratic" institutions replaced the old Communist mechanisms and supposedly lowered the costs of participation for regular citizens. This would seem to support the idea that protest would be a motivating factor for political consumerism. But Marc Morjé Howard's (2002) study of post-Communist civil society found that the echoes of both widespread distrust of government institutions and fear of brutal government response to citizen protests still provided a deterrent for citizens, keeping them from engaging in protests, at least among certain populations in post-Communist countries. Pieter Vanhuysse (2004) presents similar evidence regarding protest behavior, showing that rather than becoming more prevalent in post-Communist states, protests are not used as frequently in these nations as in other postauthoritarian countries like those in Latin America. This could lead to the belief that even a relatively anonymous "protest" action like purchasing or not purchasing a specific brand or product would be one that many citizens in post-Communist states would avoid for fear of repercussions. This contradicts the idea that political consumerism in post-Communist states would be motivated by protest politics.

However, since political consumerism can be a relatively anonymous and private mode of political participation, fear of government retaliation against citizen participation in such actions may be minimal even in post-Communist countries. In such cases, rather than shying away from political consumerism, citizens may begin to incorporate it into their normal participation repertoires at a much earlier stage than in other countries. Hence, political consumerism could become a mainstream tool in the citizen toolbox and could develop as a much stronger force in these countries than in older democracies that have a long history of creating policy change mostly through democratic institutions. All of these arguments present a puzzle about how and why post-Communist citizens would engage in political consumerism and how it fits in with existing theories about who engages in this behavior.

Examining Political Consumerism Trends Across Europe

Campaigns to boycott and buycott producers in recent years seem to be on the rise partly as a result of economic globalization and issue-specific concerns regarding sweatshops, genetically modified organisms in food, environmental degradation, pollution, and other such issues. Dietlind Stolle, Marc Hooghe, and Michele Micheletti (2005) conducted a study of World Values Survey and Political Action Survey data for industrialized democracies from 1974 to 1999 and found a fourfold increase in the number of citizens participating in boycott activity during that time. Clearly not all of the examples cited there were of direct economic consumption, per se, but they are good illustrations of ways that boycotts and other forms of political consumerism can be used to create policy change. New social surveys have broadened their spectrum in asking about political-consumerist behavior. Taking cues from other international social surveys, such as the World Values Survey, that had already been asking questions about boycotting products, the European Social Survey (ESS) incorporated two questions on political consumerism in its first-ever survey, Round 1 (2002 to 2003). The first question asked whether respondents had "boycotted certain products" in the previous twelve months. The second question asked, "During the last 12 months, have you deliberately bought certain products for political, ethical or environmental reasons?" Both questions provided response options of yes, no, don't know, no answer, or refused. Upon including both of these questions about political-consumerist behavior in Round 1, the ESS data revealed that substantial numbers of respondents in most countries had engaged in boycotts, and even more had engaged in buycotts in nearly all of the countries, even the post-Communist nations. The overview in this chapter looks at general trends of political consumerism among all respondents and also examines levels among men and women to identify if trends in post-Communist countries mirror those in more developed democracies. For a more detailed examination of trends, including those regarding conventional political activity, protest politics, and economics, see Catherine Griffiths (2009).

Figures 5.1 and 5.2 present a line graph and bar chart depicting the combined levels of both boycotts and buycotts in twenty-three countries in order from highest buycott percentage, with the four post-Communist countries clustered at one end of the chart. The overall levels of boycotts and buycotts for all countries involved in the survey are not unexpected. Long-standing European democracies with open economies and higher incomes seem to show the highest overall levels of both buycotts and boycotts. In nearly all countries, buycotts outnumbered boycotts by at least a few percentage points to as much as 25 percent. Figures 5.3 and 5.4 separately present graphs of boycott and buycott levels for several countries. Figure 5.3 shows a chart with the percentages of respondents in each country who said they had engaged in boycotting behavior within the twelve months prior to the survey, listed in order of highest

Figure 5.1 Political Consumerism by BOYcott and BUYcott Levels, ESS 2002 Data Set

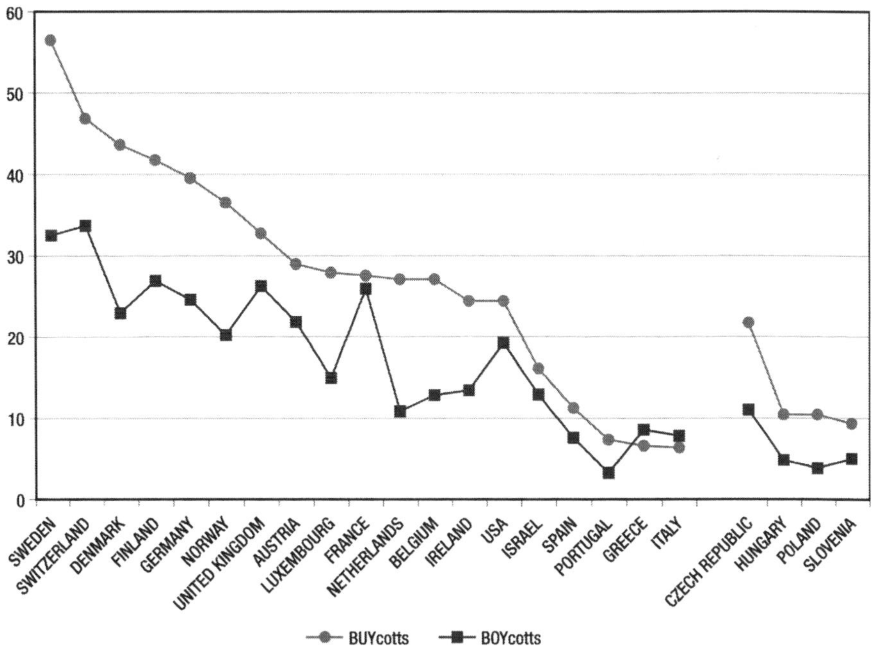

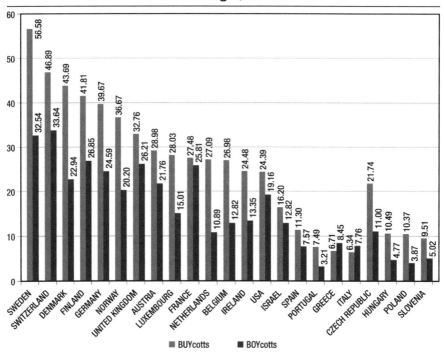

Figure 5.2 Political Consumerism by BOYcott and BUYcott Percentages, ESS 2002 Data Set

■ BUYcotts   ■ BOYcotts

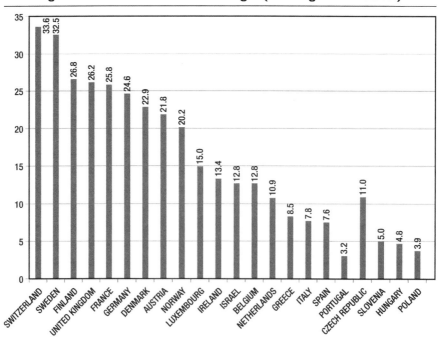

Figure 5.3 2002 BOYcott Percentages (from highest to lowest)

Figure 5.4 2002 BUYcott Percentages (from highest to lowest)

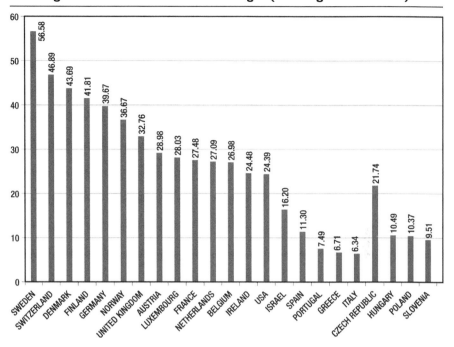

to lowest levels, with the four post-Communist countries clustered at one end. Here, two countries showed boycotting levels of greater than 30 percent (Switzerland at 33.6 percent and Sweden at 32.5 percent). Nine countries showed boycotting levels between 20 and 30 percent. Six countries show levels between 10 and 20 percent, including the Czech Republic at 11 percent. The remaining seven countries showed levels that were below 10 percent, including Slovenia (5.0 percent), Hungary (4.8 percent), and Poland (3.9 percent). In accordance with Pippa Norris's (2002b) findings, these numbers seem to support the idea that boycotting (if it is considered a protest action only) is not limited only to marginalized populations who are less fortunate financially. Most countries that showed boycott levels greater than 20 percent were older democracies with more open economies, such as Switzerland, Sweden, the United Kingdom, and Germany. For the most part, these countries seem to fit the model that protest politics is not limited to excluded and marginalized lower-income populations. This seems to indicate that a decent number of people in established, open-market nations are willing to sacrifice certain products through a boycott. Not yet answered definitively is whether they simultaneously boycott one product and replace it easily with another politically conscious product, which might have a higher price tag, suggesting that the decision might be aided by higher incomes.

The six countries where boycotting was between 10 and 20 percent appear to be a more mixed group, including a few higher-income and open-economy nations like Luxembourg and the Netherlands as well as countries like Israel and Belgium, which have less open economies. This group also includes the Czech Republic (at 11 percent). The clustering of these countries in this range of boycotts is difficult to explain without delving further into the data and will be dealt with in a separate paper. The countries at 10 percent or lower on the boycott variable include the remaining three post-Communist countries (Slovenia at 5.0 percent, Hungary at 4.8 percent, and Poland at 3.9 percent), as well as Greece (8.5 percent), Italy (7.8 percent), Spain (7.6 percent), and Portugal (3.2 percent). Based on this initial descriptive examination, it does seem somewhat relevant that many of the countries with more closed economies are post-Communist or postauthoritarian states. This could be a significant factor in whether individuals in such countries engage in boycotts. Because boycotts are typically seen as a form of protest, then, as Howard's theory suggests, individuals in postauthoritarian states may fear using that mode of political expression due to a history of political repression and severe consequences (e.g., exile, bodily harm, or death) within their country's government.

Figure 5.4 presents an overview of buycotts among twenty-two countries plus the United States, providing percentages of respondents in each country who said they had engaged in buycotting behavior within the twelve months prior to the survey, listed in order of highest to lowest levels, again with the four post-Communist countries clustered at one end. Seven of the countries, most of which are well-established democracies with strong, open economies, show figures of 30 percent or higher. In fact, in one country, Sweden, nearly 60 percent of the population had engaged in political buycotts in the past year, outpacing the nearest country by nearly ten percentage points (Switzerland at 46.89 percent). Two other countries, Denmark and Finland, both strong democracies with open markets, fell between 40 and 50 percent for buycotts. Three countries, Germany, Norway, and the United Kingdom, fell in the 30 percent range. Eight countries show levels in the 20 percent range, including the Czech Republic at 21.74 percent. This group is again a mixed crowd, including France, Ireland, Belgium, the Netherlands, Luxembourg, and Austria. Two countries, Israel and Spain, fall between 11 and 20 percent. The remaining six, including Hungary (10.49 percent), Poland (10.37 percent), and Slovenia (9.51 percent), sit at or fall below

Figure 5.5 BOYcott Levels by Gender (as % of Gender)

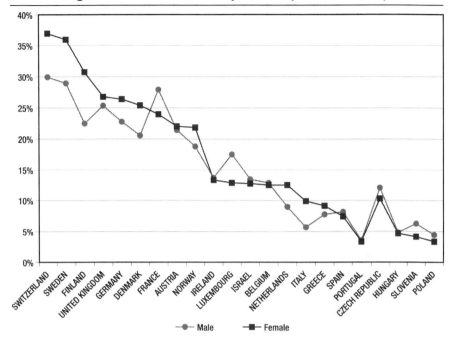

10 percent. Interestingly, the latter three countries still report levels of boycotting behavior greater than those in Portugal (7.49 percent), Greece (6.71 percent), and Italy (6.34 percent), three of the other postauthoritarian states. Overall, the trends for buycotting seem to reflect to some degree the economics argument that those in countries with higher incomes and older democracies, such as Sweden, Switzerland, Norway, the United Kingdom, and Denmark, can afford to purchase presumably higher-priced, politically conscious consumer goods that reflect their individual political, ethical, or environmental beliefs.

When it comes to gender, there seem to be some similarities among nations in terms of who boycotts and who buys. Figures 5.5–5.8 show levels of boycotting and buycotting among men and women as a percentage of their gender categories, with the post-Communist countries clustered at one end. The bar chart in Figure 5.6 shows some noticeable differences among men and women on boycotting. Figures 5.5 and 5.8 present line graphs that show more clearly the differences among male and female boycotters and buycotters. Overall, boycotts seem to occur in larger numbers in countries with long-standing democracies and open markets, which falls in line with Norris's findings in her 2002b survey.

Figure 5.6 BOYcotts by Gender (as % of Gender)

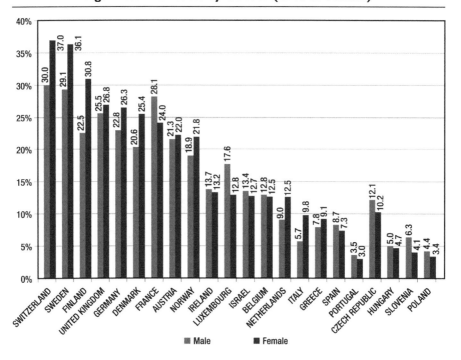

Figure 5.7 BUYcotts by Gender (as % of Gender)

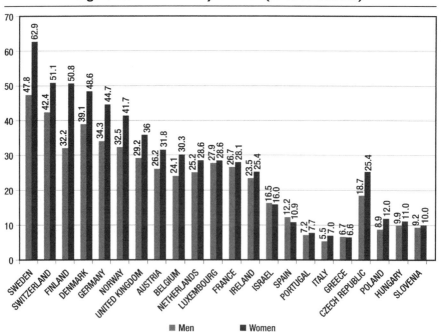

Figure 5.8 BUYcott Levels by Gender (as % of Gender)

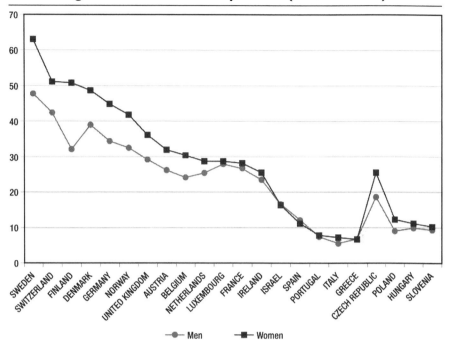

In seven countries, men either outpace or match women on boycotting behavior (Belgium, France, Ireland, Israel, Luxembourg, Portugal, and Spain). For all other countries, women engage in more boycotts than men, which contradicts the theory that men are more likely to engage in boycotts because they tend to flock to protest politics while women shy away. The post-Communist countries again fall toward the bottom of the slope in terms of overall boycotts by gender, but they present some interesting findings regarding gender and boycotts. In all such countries, men boycott more than women, though in Hungary, the levels are very close (men at 5.0 percent and women at 4.7 percent). This suggests that because boycotting is perhaps more related to protest politics, and therefore participation might incur more risks, men are more likely than women in these countries to engage in boycotting behavior. In well-established democracies, the risks of engaging in protests are much lower, so women may feel as comfortable as men in engaging in boycotts as protest without fear of governmental retribution.

In regard to buycotting and gender, Figures 5.7 and 5.8 present a bar chart and line graph, respectively, showing levels for men and women engaged in buycotting behavior. In most older open-market democracies, women outpace men by a large percentage, with Sweden leading the pack at 62.9 percent of women and only 47.8 percent of men engaging in buycotts. Three countries at the lower end of the overall levels show that men actually outnumber or match women in buycotting (Israel, Spain, and Greece). Reviewing the post-Communist countries and buycotting by gender reveals that all countries show women engaging in political buying more than men, with Czech Republic having the highest levels: women at 25.4 percent and men at 18.7 percent. Differentials between men and women in the three remaining post-Communist countries are not as large, and in Slovenia, there is less than a 1 percent difference. Still, overall data on buycotts does seem to reflect Micheletti's findings that women do engage specifically in more political buying. The reasons for that among the countries in this study have yet to be confirmed, but it could be the logical result of stereotypical gender roles. One important consideration about buycotts is that in post-Communist countries, and perhaps overall among the countries considered here, women make less money than men, but they are still more willing to spend it in political ways through positive political consumerism. This should be investigated further to see if any real relationship exists on these grounds.

Conclusion and Suggestions for Further Research

This chapter has taken an initial look at political-consumption trends emerging in post-Communist new democracies and investigated whether post-Communist democracies use marketplace consumption as a tool to express political demands and preferences in the same way that other countries do. Since this is an exploratory study of political consumption, no hard conclusions can be drawn from the data at this time. Still, some interesting patterns merit further study. While levels of political consumerism are expectedly lower in the four post-Communist countries examined here—Czech Republic, Hungary, Poland, and Slovenia— emerging trends indicate that political consumerism is finding a new home among those with an aversion to conventional political-participation methods (e.g., voting, party politics). Overall, older democracies with freer markets dominate political-consumerism trends with high levels of boycotting and even higher levels of buycotting. Again, buycott percentages were higher than boycotting in nearly every country in the study, even those post-Communist countries that were the focus of the study. The drastic political and economic transformations in post-Communist countries are providing new opportunities for citizen involvement in politics, and the modes of boycotting and buycotting may become integrated into the political-action repertoires of post-Communist citizens in a way that differs from those of long-standing democracies.

The initial findings presented here suggest several areas of future study about political consumerism and post-Communist states. One area would be the connections between political consumerism and postauthoritarianism. The data shows evidence that post-Communist Eastern European states seem to cluster with other postauthoritarian states like Spain in terms of levels of conventional political engagement and political consumerism. This suggests that the vestiges of authoritarianism have not lost strength and still hinder the political behaviors of citizens in these states. Another area for investigation is the gender differences regarding boycotting and buycotting to identify whether they are related strictly to traditional gender roles of masculine protest and feminine purchase or other factors have an impact. Finally, perhaps the most intriguing follow-up topic entails the differences among post-Communist countries in political-consumerism levels. Why does Czech Republic rank highest on boycotting and buycotting, outpacing the next country by 5 percent on boycotts and 11 percent on buycotts? Is this related to economic structure, political opportunities, government protections, or some other factor? These questions provide venues to explore in more depth the ways in which new forms of political participation are emerging in new democracies and what conditions provide the best circumstances for those new forms to develop. This chapter shows that when surveys include questions specific to engagement in political consumerism, respondents reveal their activity in such behaviors. Thus, scholars can get an expanded picture of political consumerism around the world, even in post-Communist Eastern Europe. The lesson here is that political consumerism is a budding form of participation even in the most unexpected places, where political opportunity structures are still relatively limited but expanding. These places can provide new areas of investigation for scholars working on the issue.

CHAPTER 6

TRANSNATIONAL PARTICIPATION

We are accustomed to considering political participation as occurring within the boundaries of each nation-state, but within the last generation political partici-pation across national borders has increased considerably. If, for the moment, we focus on the United States and participation stretching beyond its boundar-ies, we can remember the tremendous growth of social movements and their associated interest groups in the period from 1968 to 1974. Often using logos containing the planet Earth as a symbol, during this period groups such as the Sierra Club and the National Wildlife Federation focused preeminently on the American domestic environment and lobbying the federal government. However, as the environment, by definition, includes the entire planet, the interests and focus on the American environmental movement continually moved outward beyond national borders to encompass concerns for the fate of the rainforests and then the overarching issue of global warming. The number of transnational environmental groups thus increased from ten in 1973 to ninety in 1993 as reported in *The Yearbook of International Organizations* (Keck and Sikkink 1998, 11). This includes the emergence of Greenpeace, almost a brand name, the World Wildlife Federation, and various groups with references to the oceans or rainforests in their names. Founded in London in 1961, the transnational human rights group Amnesty International grew rapidly during the 1960s and now claims 2.8 million members worldwide (250,000 in the United States) with offices in eighty countries; it might itself be considered a brand name (see www .greenpeace.org/usa/about). The *Yearbook of International Organizations* listed

38 international human rights organizations in 1963, which had grown to 168 by 1993 (Keck and Sikkink 1998, 11). More recently, the group Transparency International was founded in Berlin in 1995 to combat political corruption worldwide and almost immediately became a force through its compilation and distribution of corruption ratings for all the governments of the world.

Nevertheless, we must show restraint in referring to "global civil society," at least with regard to the 1975–2010 period. Increasing numbers of nongovernmental organizations (NGOs) may wield increasing influence over world affairs, but the interactions of states pursuing their own interests still dominate international politics. From another perspective, transnational groups and alliances at times exercised significant influence before 1975. The abolitionist movement to end slavery, particularly among enslaved former Africans, became a worldwide movement, as Americans increasingly remember William Wilberforce and the English antislavery movement of the early nineteenth century. Similarly, after 1848 the women's movement gained a global definition, while Marxist socialists called themselves "The International." Immediately after World War II, world federalists believed that world peace depended on a world federalist state; in the early twentieth century federations of Esperanto speakers advocated a new language to enhance peace and world civilization.

Transnational political participation is an area of concern for creative participation and civic innovation. In terms of the definition of participation as civic innovation and the construction of new political forms, much transnational participation involves citizens concerned with threats to the planet's common-pool resources, such as global warming or the depletion of forests, but such individuals are scattered across national boundaries. Many issues of transnational participation involve scattered individuals concerned with commonweal goals. In addition, almost by definition, transnational political participation relies on the construction of new forms of public action, lacking in the existing political forms embodied within the institutions bounded by the nation-state. This puts a premium on creative participation, such as Amnesty International's enjoining individual members to write letters to particular prisoners in foreign countries where incarceration violates human rights norms or its constructing international fora open to all who wish to discuss and debate problems of neoliberal world organization.

A number of interesting cases of transnational political participation are discussed below. The boycott of the Swiss conglomerate Nestlé from 1977 to 1984 is something of an archetype of transnational political consumerism directed against a multinational corporation. In this instance, protesters charged that Nestlé promoted the substitution of baby formula for breast milk in Third World countries, which often have unsanitary drinking water, thereby creating severe health risks for babies. Nearly twenty years later, the Brent Spar incident (1995) led to a huge volume of protest against Shell Oil in Germany, Denmark, the Netherlands, and Norway, with support orchestrated by Greenpeace in the United Kingdom and elsewhere. Shell Oil announced that the Brent Spar storage platform in the North Sea, no longer needed, would be towed out into the North Atlantic and dropped to the ocean floor. Greenpeace protested and publicized Shell's plan, and television pictures of the suppression of protests led to a huge, spontaneous anti-Shell boycott in Germany and other countries neighboring the North Sea.

Beginning in the early 1990s, boycott threats against Nike and other shoe and clothing manufacturers received great attention in the United States and Western Europe. Most American shoes were being imported from China, Indonesia, Vietnam, and other Asian countries. The new issue became whether shoes, clothing, soccer equipment, and other imported consumer items were being manufactured by workers paid only a pittance, while often subject to unhealthy factory conditions. Stemming from such concerns about manufacturing and the destruction of common-pool resources like rainforests, eco-labels were established and have sometimes been influential, particularly in Europe, since the early 1990s. The purpose of eco-labels is to influence consumers' purchasing decisions by indicating that a product has been manufactured under adequate labor standards or using wood not lumbered from ecologically endangered primeval forests. Particularly well-known in the United States is "fair-trade" labeling on coffee products, indicating that the coffee has been grown by small farmers who follow ecologically beneficial agricultural practices. Obviously such labels have varying degrees of authenticity, depending upon the inspection agency issuing permission for them.

In a world of sovereign nation-states, it is truly difficult for scattered citizens to organize to protest government corruption in countries other than their own; yet, such corruption can have a great impact on the effective implementation of environmental policies affecting the entire planet. Since 1995, however, it has been possible to support the efforts of Transparency International, which has established local branches in seventy countries, as it attempts to reduce governmental corruption by publicizing its relative incidence in countries around the world (see Transparency International website at www.transparency.org).

Advocacy Networks

Margaret E. Keck and Kathryn Sikkink's landmark work in political science. *Activists Beyond Borders: Advocacy Networks in International Politics* (1998), has established basic concepts for the understanding of transnational political participation. The book makes its first point in the title: Advocacy networks are the basis for transnational political activism. In most cases of concern here, a communications network extending across national boundaries must be established. Persons at nodes within the network communicate about mutual goals and public actions to further them, as well as about where and when such actions can be organized. Since about 1995, the Internet has served as the nerve center of such communications networks; before then, of course, action was quite possible through international telephone communication, air travel, and the mail; before that there were the mail, underwater cables, and steamships.

In the transnational advocacy network, somewhere a group will start a committee for public action on some transnational issue. The original committee will spark the creation of branches or of coequal committees across national boundaries. In some situations, the component units of the network are created anew, as in committees for the Nestlé boycott. But more commonly, they are preexisting groups, usually particular to a specific country. Depending upon the issue and nation, component units of the network may be local environmental groups, political parties, interest groups, churches, labor unions, student organizations, women's groups, and other civil-society groups, which appoint representatives to the committee for their particular country and simultaneously communicate with the transnational network. Indeed, units of government, for instance, parliaments and parliamentary committees, local agencies, and specialized bureaucratic groups such as environmental agencies or health regulators, may select agents to participate in the network. A few participants in transnational advocacy networks may be affiliated with regional organizations (such as inter-American national groups) or international organizations, including specialized agencies such as the World Health Organization (WHO). The public actions of such networks have frequently targeted the World Bank, International Monetary Fund (IMF), and World Trade Organization (WTO).

Transnational political participation as creative participation does rely upon advocacy networks, indicating an overlap between ideas of participation and representation. Individuals for a common cause who are scattered around the planet rely upon "advocates" (or representatives) communicating with one another among clusters of committees. Such representation does have its disappointing aspects. Being part of a transnational representative network limits an individual's own public action. But there is little alternative if the individual is to have any effectiveness at all. It is ordinarily not possible to bring together global citizens to interact face-to-face and discuss how to influence some government, likely not related to most participants, to take some action of value to individuals across the planet.

The Boomerang

After stressing the importance of advocacy networks in transnational participation, Keck and Sikkink (1998, 12–31) emphasize the importance of the "boomerang" strategy. This is another example of the one-step-removed effects in international participation. The boomerang refers to the strategy of influencing one's own government to act against a second-party government to change one or more of its policies. A classic example in the political science literature involves U.S. civil rights groups pressuring Congress to act against South African apartheid, while domestic advocacy groups in France, the United Kingdom, and Australia also pressured their governments to act against the policy. Such multiple "boomerangs" apparently became a significant catalyst for the 1989 change in the South African regime (Klotz 1995). There are basically two types of boomerang participation with about equal significance in relation to one another from a worldwide perspective. The first, as just indicated, entails acting through previously established political groups to influence one's own government to act against a third party. Another mode of participation is acting through transnational advocacy networks to persuade one's own government, or one or more foreign governments, to act against a third party. In many cases, significant new international coordinating committees may be created for public action on a transnational issue. For instance, in the early 1990s, as the preservation of Brazilian rainforests became an international issue, new international coordinating committees were created to influence American and Western European governments to influence Brazilian national policy on the issue (Keck and Sikkink 1998, 136–147).

From the standpoint of creative participation in transnational action, a first step is the initial formation of an environmental group, which at least in the United States, involves organizing scattered individuals through mail or Internet solicitation. This can be characterized as a joint expression of social-movement and civic-innovative participation. If a preexisting domestic environmental group moves to act abroad through the boomerang strategy, this is a further expression of civic innovation in tandem with social movements, as political action is taken beyond traditional institutional means of expression. A more intense expression of civic innovation is the creation of an environmental group, expected to act at once transnationally, as was the case with Greenpeace in 1971. Local chapters of Greenpeace can be expected to pressure their own national governments to act in boomerang fashion, although this strategy may vary in effectiveness; for instance, in my judgment Greenpeace has not been one of the top five influential environmental lobbies in Washington, D.C. (Bosso 2005, 101–102). It is an act of civic innovation and creative participation to establish a transnational advocacy network on some issue or group of issues, such as preserving primordial forests in the planet's equatorial regions. But a second form of transnational creative participation does not involve the boomerang strategy, at least not directly. This is political consumerism, extending across national boundaries and directed against a multinational corporation, such as Nestlé or Shell Oil. In other words, sometimes a transnational advocacy network coordinates a boycott and other political actions directed against a corporation seen as offending a commonweal goal. Actually, in the Brent Spar case, a spontaneous boycott occurred after televised demonstrations by Greenpeace. On other occasions, an international committee might sponsor a label to encourage shoppers to buy a product beneficial to the planetary commonweal. Fair-trade labels for coffee, shoes, and wood products are forms of action directly linked to the marketplace and not seen as immediately acting to influence governments. This is a marketplace strategy, not a boomerang strategy.

Transnational boycotts must be appreciated for what they are. International corporations with yearly sales of $1 billion, let alone oil companies with $100 billion in annual sales, are not likely to change their policies in light of some possible slight drop in revenues inspired by political consumerism. The real name of the game is a boycott's threat to the corporate brand (Vogel 2005, 42–44, 53). An international corporation may spend tens of millions per year in advertising to enhance its brand name. Why? In the very long run, they do this to increase sales, thus profits, and this period is expected to last much longer than that of slight drops in sales caused by a boycott. The international corporation's more immediate goal is to protect its political position, which in the long run relates to profits. An international oil corporation, for instance, must be regarded as sufficiently public spirited to receive drilling leases from governments outside its homeland. In the United States, an international oil company has likely received special tax breaks for expensive drilling in the Gulf of Mexico and elsewhere, and it does not want to become politically unpopular with, then targeted by, congressional Democrats looking for new sources of funds. Many types of corporations desire a trustworthy reputation in public statements about corporate environmental policy, especially when petitioning governments to lessen environmental regulation of production practices. Of course, a popular brand name is not just a means of political protection, although this is especially true for oil companies. The makers of Tide want me to react favorably to the Tide brand name, so that when I shop at Target (itself a brand name with a logo), I will buy their $16 twelve-pound box of detergent, rather than Surf, a no-name brand, selling for $13 a box.

The major point of a transnational consumer boycott, then, is that it threatens the credibility of a corporate brand name. Publicity about the boycott probably will not result in a significant drop in sales and profits, in the short run at least, but corporate decision makers are likely to see it as harmful to the brand name because they allocate tens of millions to advertising agencies for brand promotion. Consequently, a transnational boycott or consumer campaign of criticism can lead to some change in the corporate policy of a multi-billion-dollar enterprise.

Boycotts and particular demonstrations sometimes have expanded into "adversarial advocacy networks" directed against a large multinational corporation. For instance, anti-Nestlé boycotts have been conducted repeatedly since 1977, while calls for protests against ExxonMobil have been continuous since the proliferation of Internet usage around 1995. A number of large multinational corporations are now subject to criticism from adversarial networks that, while shifting in nature and composition, are perhaps permanent. Such adversarial networks are directed against Nestlé, Shell Oil, ExxonMobil, Walmart, Microsoft, Nike, and probably others as a Google search will indicate. The two anti-Walmart groups are based in American unions, such as the Service and Food Workers Union and the United Food and Commercial Workers (see www.WakeUpWalMart.com); the others are instances of civic innovation and creative participation. The political scientist need not accept the stated reasons for nonstop opposition to these multinational corporations to take interest in this unusual form of political participation. In general, this introductory picture of transnational political participation, with its advocacy networks, boomerang strategies, Internet coordination by committee, boycotts, threats against brand names, and positive labeling points to a form of political participation that, while not entirely new, is growing in importance.

Such growth is due to processes now familiarly captured by the term "globalization," meaning the great increase in the volume of international trade and the mutual influences among nations regarding economic policies and regulation. In addition to the international trade factors, more people in more countries are becoming concerned about limited planetary common-pool resources and the need for transnational public action to preserve them and to combat global warming. However, this does not mean that an intensely organized, global civil society is emerging. Creative participation in transnational political action often seems to have some impact on government and corporate policies, but in such cases like the boycotts of Nestlé and ExxonMobil, transnational political participation has a quite limited effect.

The Nestlé Boycott

The international boycott of the Swiss multinational corporation's household grocery goods is among the best-known transnational political consumer actions. (My account is largely drawn from S. Prakash Sethi [1994] and some of the group web pages, such as www.ibfan.org and www.babymilkaction.org). The anti-Nestlé boycott started in 1977, was called off from 1981 to 1984, and resumed in 1988, although with less force than in the 1977–1981 period. An international boycott against Nestlé continues today, spearheaded by the International Baby Food Action Network (IBFAN), which seems to have some effect in the United Kingdom, although not much elsewhere. This illustrates a problem with the boycott as a political strategy. It is usually hard to discern a clear-cut end to a consumer boycott; such actions often simply dwindle to a barely observable level after a few years, thereby discrediting the entire boycott effort as ineffective. In the Nestlé situation, a well-organized international committee called off the initial boycott in 1984 after judging Nestlé to have acceded to its demands. Issues with implementation of the agreement with Nestlé led to the reinstitution of the boycott in 1988, with boycotting actions continuing ever since then.

The main issue in the anti-Nestlé boycott has been the international corporation's actions in selling baby formula for bottle feeding as a replacement for breast milk in Third World countries. The main concern has been that the use of contaminated local water in formula preparation could kill babies due to the prevalence of bacteria causing killer dysentery. Furthermore, impoverished mothers may dilute the formula to an excessive degree, leading to malnutrition, and formula does not contain antigens and nutrients found in breast milk that are necessary to babies' good health.

Thus, according to a commitment to worldwide human rights or to Christianity, Judaism, and other moral standards common in Europe and North America, safeguards must be established to regulate the marketing patterns of baby formula by Western corporations selling the product in the Third World. But in the early 1970s, this was a new and unforeseen issue as there was an institutional gap in dealing with it. The WHO and other international organizations did not immediately take up the issue of regulating Nestlé and other international corporations' sales practices for baby formula. National governments did not start to take action.

The international issue-framing process began with the publication in August 1973 of an article titled "The Baby Food Tragedy" in a British periodical, the *New Internationalist*. The article was based on an interview with two medical child-care specialists, who claimed that the marketing of baby formula was promoting disease among Third World babies. The article singled out Nestlé for its aggressive marketing practices, and 3,000 copies were sent to Third World hospitals. Nestlé defended its position in the October 1973 issue of the *New Internationalist* but could do little else to defend itself. A few months later, in March 1974, a more pointed attack on Nestlé was published as *The Baby Killer*, written by Mike Muller and published by the London-based NGO War on Want, an advocate for poverty issues in the Third World. *The Baby Killer* accused Nestlé and other corporations of causing disease and death by marketing baby formula as a substitute for breast milk. In May 1974, the pamphlet was translated into German by a small committee known as the Third World Action Group (TWAG) and distributed in Switzerland, Nestlé's home territory. Nestlé immediately sued TWAG for libel. Hearings were held in Berne in November 1975 and February and June 1976. The judge found thirty members of TWAG guilty of libel and fined each 300 Swiss francs (then US$150). But this was not a major punishment, and the judge criticized Nestlé, stating, "The need ensues for the Nestlé Company to fundamentally rethink its advertising practices in developing countries as concerns bottle feeding" (Sethi 1994, 51–56).

Technically Nestlé won the libel case, but politically the case was a disaster. The trial was of natural interest to the media, which promulgated the charges against Nestlé. Activists in the United States catalyzed transnational political action. The National Council of Churches in reaction to the civil rights movement in the late 1960s had formed the Interfaith Committee on Social Responsibility, which became in 1973 the Interfaith Center on Corporate Responsibility (ICCR). Although originally oriented toward poverty issues in the United States, activists within the ICCR became concerned about the role of corporations in the Third World. The issue of Nestlé injuring babies was of obvious concern to ICCR activists, and a group in the Minneapolis, Minnesota, area founded a spin-off group to act against Nestlé, the Infant Formula Action Committee (INFACT). INFACT staged a major demonstration against Nestlé on July 4, 1977, in Minneapolis, launching an effective campaign to boycott Nestlé through preexisting networks of church-affiliated reform activists, presumably mostly from the more social liberal Protestant congregations, together with some activist priests and nuns. The issue of Nestlé's injuring babies through its marketing practices was an extraordinarily stark one, easily framed in black-and-white terms, while INFACT had the services of a few activists skilled in publicity. In May 1978, Senator Ted Kennedy became interested in the issue and held a hearing in which baby-formula distributors made a poor impression.

The baby-formula issue and criticism of Nestlé had originated in Western Europe, where other committees were formed to boycott the corporation. Anti-Nestlé publicity reached the level at which institutions took up the issue. The staffs of the WHO and UNICEF convened an international meeting on infant and child feeding in Geneva in October 1979, which concluded with the suggestion that the WHO issue "an international code of marketing of infant formula" (Sethi 1994, 179). The next meeting of the World Health Assembly in May 1980 instructed staff to prepare such a marketing code, which the WHO assembly endorsed in May 1981 by a vote of 115–1–3 (the Ronald Reagan administration cast the sole negative vote, indicating its free market perspective). The detailed WHO market code would serve as strict regulation if actually implemented. It prohibited the advertising of baby formula to the general public, distribution of free samples, special displays, discount coupons, premiums, special sales, and loss leaders. The code forbade marketers from making contact with pregnant women to sell their product. It did allow the industry to give hospitals free samples of baby formula, but only the hospitals themselves could distribute the samples. The code also forbade the industry from making gifts to health-care workers and regulated labeling practices. Member states ratifying the code would assume responsibility for enforcing it, while the WHO would collect information about enforcement.

The code was sufficient to meet activists' goals but was not well implemented. Few nations immediately ratified it. After the initial WHO-UNICEF meeting in

1979, the activist cause was furthered by IBFAN, a coalition adding European protest groups to the American groups. Also in 1979, the International Nestlé Boycott Committee was formed for transnational coordination (Sethi 1994, 165–166). This international coordinating committee did step up pressure to enforce the WHO code, but it was insufficient to gain widespread implementation. Meanwhile, the IBFAN-led Nestlé boycott and protest continued. According to interviews by S. Prakash Sethi, by late 1980 the Swiss leadership of Nestlé had become concerned about the corporation's political vulnerability in the United States (although later the Reagan administration supported Nestlé), even though, despite "all the public hue and cry, Nestlé's global operations had not suffered noticeable loss of revenue" (1994, 219). In August 1981, Nestlé formed a subsidiary, the Nestlé Coordinating Center for Nutrition, to develop a strategy to halt boycotts and criticism of the corporation. This group in turn formed the Nestlé Infant Formula Audit Commission, chaired by former senator Edmund Muskie of Maine, which turned out actually to be independent in auditing Nestlé's actions under the WHO infant-formula marketing code. Some of the religious leaders of the boycott became convinced of Nestlé's emerging good faith, and after about three years of tense negotiations, in April 1984 Nestlé issued a statement outlining a code of conduct for its marketing of infant formula similar to the one issued by the WHO. At this point the international committee called off the boycott, becoming one case in which a transnational advocacy network clearly terminated a boycott action. (The IBFAN reinstituted a boycott against Nestlé in 1988; this was a new action led by a different group. See the IBFAN webpage under the headings "The Issue" and "History of the Campaign.")

We can judge the anti-Nestlé boycott as somewhat successful in that it persuaded the corporation of the need to self-regulate some of its marketing processes. This was evident in 1984; current information is not available, although we can state hypotheses. One would expect some reversion to unregulated marketing practices as the years wear on as no institution exists with strict powers to regulate baby-formula marketing. On the other hand, the Nestlé case is exceptional in that a long-lasting adversarial network has developed against the corporation. At present this network is focused on a British group, Baby Milk Action, affiliated with the worldwide IBFAN, which still exists. In the twenty-first century, Nestlé continues to face pressure in the United Kingdom from protests organized by Baby Milk Action. The Internet indicates a significant amount of organizing about the baby-formula issue continues in Britain. The relatively permanent anti-Nestlé network would seem to exercise a degree of power over the corporation.

In other words, Nestlé must strive to implement the WHO code to some degree or face negative publicity arising from appeals to WHO, European Union regulatory bodies, or the U.S. Congress when majority Democrats can schedule public hearings. Concerns about the brand name persist; for instance, Perrier is a Nestlé brand, and protests forced Nestlé to discontinue a Perrier-sponsored award ceremony for British comedians. The corporation continued to experience image problems as late as 2005; an online opinion poll yielding 15,500 responses worldwide indicated that Nestlé, Nike, Coca Cola, and McDonald's were the corporations most frequently targeted by the 36 percent claiming they had boycotted a company (of course this is not a random group) (Tran 2005).

The Nestlé boycott can be considered creative participation as civic innovation. In this instance, scattered people concerned about an injustice initially lacked established institutions for public action, especially as the target of action was headquartered in Switzerland. Religion and humanitarian activists succeeded in creating vehicles for transnational action. The pathway was unusual; the protest group criticized the multinational corporation, thereby framing an issue and generating worldwide publicity. This got the attention of the staffs of international organizations, which, in consultation with national delegates, issued a code of behavior for multinational corporations in a particular area of economic activity. After this, public action had to focus on the implementation process of influencing businesses to follow the code of behavior. In this instance, the adversarial advocacy coalition became semipermanent, creating a mechanism to protest egregious violations of the marketing code to institutions having political influence. Ordinary citizens could continue to participate in the advocacy network, especially in Britain, by making monetary contributions, attending protest demonstrations, boycotting, communicating through social-networking sites, signing Internet petitions, writing or e-mailing members of Parliament, distributing literature from booths at public events, and requesting that wholefood grocery stores drop Nestlé products. Ordinary citizens can thus feel that they are participating in an international action and that such international activity has some influence on events.

The Brent Spar Incident

The Brent Spar incident of 1995 is possibly the major event in European environmental action by agencies other than the state.[1] As a result of the incident, the term "political consumerism" was coined to refer to research by Danish economists before Michele Micheletti and others further defined the concept (Instituttet for Fremtidsforsning and Elsam 1996). In the Brent Spar incident, outraged consumers in Germany, Denmark, the Netherlands, and several other countries responded to television footage of Greenpeace demonstrations on the Brent Spar oil platform in the North Sea, as Greenpeace sought to block Shell Oil from disposing of the platform in the North Atlantic. Americans remain surprisingly unaware of this environmental event.

Brent Spar was an oil-storage facility used by Shell and Esso in the North Sea oil field, halfway between the Shetlands and Norway. A large maritime structure, 90 feet above and 360 feet below water, it consisted of storage tanks held together by a steel framework. "Spar" is a technical term for a maritime platform structure held in place by tethers to concrete anchors on the ocean floor. In this case, it is important to visualize the Brent Spar as a structure of hollow tanks for the purpose of storing crude oil. One can thus readily imagine the spar's being untethered from the bottom, then towed through the sea to a disposal location.

The Brent Spar was constructed in 1976 to store the oil drawn from the drilling rigs in the Brent oil field in the North Sea. However, after an oil pipeline was constructed to the Shetland Islands, by 1991 the Brent Spar had outlived its usefulness and was shut down. It was operated by Shell Oil, which under maritime law was responsible for removing it from the seas after it was no longer in use. In 1994, Shell studied two different disposal possibilities—in the sea or on land. Shell's study favored the sea-disposal route, which not only saved £20 million over land disposal but was arguably environmentally superior. The storage tank had been damaged during the 1976 installation, and the fear was that it might burst during the moving process. Sea disposal would entail sinking the spar to a depth of perhaps 2.5 kilometers, which it was hoped would not harm the ocean floor beyond the immediate vicinity. Towing to Scotland or Norway, on the other hand, might involve greater environmental damage if an accident occurred in shallow coastal waters. Further, the process of rendering the spar vertical while towing it onto land, then disassembling it would have negative environmental impacts. Therefore, Shell applied to the British government for permits to tow the spar to the North Atlantic in British waters and to sink it there.

However, from Greenpeace's perspective, a spar should be towed to land. Greenpeace, a transnational environmental group founded in 1971 in Vancouver and headquartered in Amsterdam after 1989, claimed 2.8 million members worldwide in 1995. (This may be an exaggeration, but Greenpeace certainly had many contributors.) More than most environmental groups, Greenpeace had focused on maritime issues and used maritime strategies, as in the famous example of small Greenpeace boats interfering with whale harpooning. In particular, Greenpeace had developed a negative frame for "dumping" pollution and waste in the ocean. From its perspective, solid waste material should never be dumped in the ocean and must be moved to land, where steel and other materials can be recycled.

The disposal issue was initially controlled by Shell UK, which had a favorable relationship with the government of John Majors, Margaret Thatcher's Conservative Party successor. Until the very end, the Majors cabinet backed the Shell proposal to dispose of the spar in the North Atlantic. Accordingly, Shell UK paid no attention to public opinion in Germany, Denmark, and the Netherlands, some of the nations bordered by the North Sea. However, in these countries, the issue of polluting the North Sea was a matter of top environmental concern after a major previous controversy over the proper disposal of industrial wastes dumped into the Rhine River by manufacturers concentrated in the Rhine basin.

It came as no surprise, then, that after Shell Oil's disposal plan was announced on February 16, 1995, Greenpeace's international leadership decided in Amsterdam on April 11 to act to stop the "ocean dumping" of the Brent Spar and to get Shell Oil to dispose of the facility on land. Greenpeace had the resources to create a media-publicized occupation of Brent Spar; it also had the money to rent a yacht for £20,000, pay the demonstrators for their time, and purchase other supplies. The organization had twenty-four years of experience in organizing to occupy, or sail into, spaces to disrupt economic activity and was also versed in gaining attention from television news. Ten activists disembarked from two Greenpeace boats on April 30 and occupied the spar until they were removed on May 23 by Shell security (with police observers). Greenpeace then managed to get to television news producers a few pictures of the removal process that made Shell security look like fascists. A second disruption occurred on June 7 as five activists reoccupied the spar but were removed by Shell on June 10. Although fire-hosed water from Shell boats flipped over two Greenpeace rubber rafts, spilling occupants into the sea, no pictures of this were caught for television. On the whole, the two disruptions were only minor successes. There was some news treatment in the United Kingdom, but not a lot. Just as Greenpeace had twenty-four years of experience with demonstrations, so the news media also had twenty-four years of experience covering environmentalist protests, and such demonstrations were no longer considered priority news, especially if they lacked dramatic photos, which did not appear until the first removal day (Jordan 2001, 149–154).

On June 11, 1995, Shell began to tow the Brent Spar to the disposal site, setting off a firestorm of public criticism in Germany, Denmark, and the Netherlands that led to an end of the ocean disposal plan on June 20. Greenpeace followed the tow in its boat, but its dinghies and efforts to attach banners were again met with fire hoses. On June 16 and 20, attempts were made to drop activists onto the spar from a helicopter. The Shell boats directed fire hose streams in the direction of the Greenpeace helicopter, creating extraordinarily dramatic pictures for television news. This essentially doomed Shell's effort (Jordan 2001, 155). After the May 23 removal of the occupiers and subsequent television and print coverage, millions of German, Danish, and Dutch consumers became disgusted with Shell and spontaneously boycotted Shell gasoline. Greenpeace later claimed to have organized the boycott, but scholarly description of the incident indicates it was a spontaneous expression of mass disgust, not really organized by a central body (Jordan 2001, 164–165, 179–180). A Shell petrol station was fire-bombed in the week after June 11, and threats were made to blow up other Shell stations on the continent. The head of Shell Austria announced that he did not support the corporate decision; the head of Shell Germany publicly supported the decision but privately and aggressively sought a meeting to reverse the ocean-disposal decision, as Shell's German consumer operations faced collapse (Jordan 2001, 168). The boycott of petrol stations can be more effective than most consumer boycotts because customers can normally purchase the same product for the same price in the immediate vicinity. Finally, at a meeting in The Hague, near corporate headquarters, on June 20, Shell's international leadership suspended the towing operation and changed the disposal policy to seeking a land site. Greenpeace and a consumer boycott had defeated Shell (Jordan 2001, 178).

The Brent Spar was towed to a temporary location on the Norwegian coast, and in 1998, Shell and the Norwegian government agreed that it could be towed to the Stavanger area, placed on its side, and serve as a base for a roll-on, roll-off ferry terminal. A few months later in 1998, a meeting of the maritime regulatory body for the North Sea, the Oslo and Paris Convention and Commission (normally referred to as OSPAR) ruled that larger drilling rigs must be disposed of on land, although exceptions were made for smaller rigs and some unusual structures. In the opinion of many, the environmental advantage of land disposal of North Sea rigs is questionable, and there is a strong case that

OSPAR made this decision based on public opinion in Germany, Denmark, and the Netherlands, rather than technical analysis (Jordan 2001, 191–229). (Shell faced less criticism in the United Kingdom and Norway.)

The Greenpeace occupation and spontaneous consumer boycott thus defeated Shell and were influential in institutionalizing the environmental position with an international maritime regulator. While describing the boycott as spontaneous, I note that before the June 11 tow, several European governmental leaders, including the Swedish and Danish environmental ministers and the European Union commissioner for the environment, publicly criticized the towing plan (Jordan 2001, 164, 166). After June 11, German establishment organizations, such as "a major Protestant church meeting in Hamburg," the metalworkers' union, and the national newspaper *Bild*, called for a boycott of Shell (Jordan 2001, 168). A television poll indicated that two-thirds of Germans surveyed claimed to be boycotting Shell. Political scientist Grant Jordan collected the following German headlines from June 14 and 15: "Shell stands in the firing line" (*Recklinghauser Zeitung*); "Shell petrol stations shut" (*Weser Kurier*); "Indignation and rage about Shell" (*Oranienburger Generalanzeiger*); "Giant wave of boycotts puts Shell under pressure" (*Schwabische Donauzeitung*) (Jordan 2001, 168, 175).

The massive consumer protest in Germany exemplifies creative participation and civic innovation. Millions of Germans came together to boycott Shell to reflect a disposition for immediate public action to defend the integrity of the ocean, a public good. As early as May 29, Angela Merkel, the then German environmental minister, had expressed a preference for on-land disposal of North Sea rigs, but the German public could not wait for its government to try to pressure the Majors cabinet, which had already declared its complete support for Shell's disposal plan (Jordan 2001, 165). I would refer to this massive public action for commonweal goals as creative participation, rather than action by an environmental movement, because the protest was basically an action by the entire politically aware German public. However, different modes of political participation are often connected, so I would say that creative participation was linked to the previous public action by Greenpeace, a social-movement organization.

Greenpeace suffered damage to its own brand name, despite its ability to claim victory in the Brent Spar incident. A key issue in the disposal controversy entailed the amount of oil remaining in the spar's tanks. Shell initially stated the amount was 53 tons, but Greenpeace later claimed that 1,450 tons of oil remained. However, a neutral Norwegian commission later found only 74 to 103 tons of oil, essentially validating Shell's position (Jordan 2001, 134). Greenpeace was forced to issue an apology for its inaccurate statement, maintaining that it resulted from a necessarily hasty observation by its occupiers. An immediate argument against environmental positions charges that environmentalists' facts are normally inaccurate, and Greenpeace's inaccuracy in the Brent Spar incident damaged its image in Europe, where its reputation as a protector of the environment had been greater than in the United States (Micheletti 2003, 82, 152). On the other hand, Shell Oil suffered damage to its brand name in Europe as Shell looked like a defeated Goliath. Subsequently, Shell has been targeted by a number of calls for boycotts and protests over issues such as oil drilling in the Nigerian delta, activity in human rights violator Myanmar (Burma), and gas pipeline construction in northwestern Ireland. Of course, this means that Shell must devote significant attention to public-relations campaigns seeking to indicate its concern for the common good.

Clothing, Shoes, and the Third World

In the United States, a central trend in participation in world clothing and shoe markets is epitomized by criticisms of the Nike brand shoe, leading to the organization of two national NGO committees in 1988, the Fair Labor Association (FLA) and the Worker Rights Consortium (WRC) (Micheletti 2003, 1, 12–14, 83, 84, 97, 177–178; Greenhouse 1998; FLA and WRC websites at www.fairlabor.org and www.workersrights.org). These NGOs seek to promote and enforce labor and factory codes for the manufacture of imported clothing and shoes into the United States.

In the late 1980s and early 1990s, American shoe fashions changed with the popularity of a new type of athletic shoe. The newly founded Nike corporation became the most popular athletic shoe manufacturer in the United States, attaining 40 percent of the market. This was partly due to one of the most successful advertising campaigns in the history of consumer products, emblematized by the Nike "swoosh" logo and the slogan "Just do it." Nike led the way in gaining endorsements from leading athletes, including Michael Jordan, perhaps the United States' most popular sports figure. However, Nike was manufacturing its shoes cheaply in Indonesia, Vietnam, and China, buying from contractors and subcontractors who sometimes used child labor, paying extremely low wages, and operating unsanitary factories. Because Nike was garnering a great degree of attention from youths and others in its extraordinary advertising campaign, and because it was promoting itself as a new and "cool" product, it opened itself to media exposure for promoting slave-wage conditions, an American media tradition dating back at least to the Progressive era. Exposures of Nike were printed in *Life* and *Time* and appeared on Kathy Lee Gifford's daytime television talk show (Vogel 2005, 78; Saporito 1998).

Meanwhile, organized labor was happy to work with activist student networks to expose substandard working conditions in the manufacture of imported clothing, particularly the college and university logo clothing that had become another fashion trend in the late 1980s (and been standard ever since). Child labor and substandard wages were also issues for the type of internationally oriented religious activists who supported the Nestlé boycott (Vogel 2005, 71–86).

At the same time President Bill Clinton was contemplating running for reelection, after offending half of the Democrats in Congress and most labor-union supporters by initiating the North American Free Trade Agreement. Accordingly, Clinton sought to deal with the international labor issue by convening the White House Apparel Industry Partnership (AIP) in April 1996. Nike and seventeen other major clothing importers, along with unions and human rights NGOs, were persuaded to participate in the AIP, a committee to develop a code for the manufacture of imported clothing and shoes and then to certify products with a label indicating their manufacture according to fair-labor standards. In 1988, however, the AIP group split into two groups, largely over the issue of requiring payment of a "living wage," supported by unions and human rights groups, as opposed to the local "prevailing wage," which might be so low as not to meet definitions of a "living wage." Unions pulled out of the FLA and with supporters formed the WRC, which emphasized fair wages (Vogel 2005, 78, 82–83). Each group claimed about 180 college and university members by 2005; most of these joined both the FLA and the WRC. It appears that the more stringent WRC regulations placed more attention on college and university licensing practices for the use of their logos.

Both groups set up impartial monitoring systems for the factories contracting to Nike and other clothing importers subscribing to the FLA and WRC. Apparently the formation of these organizations, at least for a while, eliminated many of the more egregious violations of child-labor and safety standards in major contracting factories in East Asia. However, the implementation of such fair-labor codes in practice has tended to decline, in this case because many of the larger Asian enterprises looked to move to new and still cheaper manufacturing areas, such as Cambodia and Bangladesh. In addition, FLA and WRC standards could be circumvented by subcontracting work to small manufacturers (often owned by Korean entrepreneurs), which were particularly difficult to locate and inspect. Further, critics noted that the on-site inspectors were not manufacturing experts but inexperienced young people contracting for the job.

The FLA and WRC are transnational organizations, even though most of their board members are domestic American organizations, although a few NGOs are represented. They are thus primarily American coordinating committees aiming to influence industrial practices in foreign countries, that is, to exercise transnational power. Their formation blends creative participation and action with established political institutions, such as the American presidency and textile-industry unions. Students' and religious activists' civic-innovation protests occurred side by side with union protests and were rapidly absorbed into the political system in 1996 by the Clinton political organization. This illustrates the idea of "balanced participation" in which public action occurs simultaneously in established institutions and newly created groups.

The idea of the AIP might be called "cooperative pluralism" in that negotiators from corporations, unions, and NGOs were to find common ground in developing factory codes for manufacturers of imported clothing and shoes (McFarland 1993). Cooperative pluralism entails the attempt to find common ground among adversaries. The normal criticism of cooperative pluralism is that if government is not part of the negotiating body, no authoritative institution exists to enforce the common-ground agreements reached by negotiators. However, the case of the AIP, FLA, and WRC can be viewed against the previous discussion of political consumerism. These private labor-standards labeling bodies clearly have a huge problem in implementing their rules and making sure that foreign factories are following them. In this situation, there is a sanction (if rather weak in most cases) that popular clothing and shoe brands want to protect their brand name, and negative publicity from factory code violations does injure a brand name.

Coffee and Fair Trade

After World War II, an increasing number of scattered individuals in North America and Western Europe became concerned with the economic plight of citizens in the underdeveloped economies of the world, those nations referred to as the Third World. Such individuals may be motivated by compassion and likely believe that dollar-a-day families are suffering due to an unjust distribution of income worldwide. They likely support Franklin Roosevelt's statement that one of the four freedoms central to human rights is "freedom from want." At first such scattered individuals would see no means of public action to alleviate Third World poverty beyond the insufficient aid given by Western governments, mainly intent on countering the spread of Soviet and Chinese communism. Such people then acted and participated in forms of civic innovation, which regard the *civitas* as the entire world. In the following discussion, I focus on the United States, then on the phenomenon of transnational fair trade in the production and distribution of coffee.

As shown in *Activists Beyond Borders*, in the sphere of transnational political participation people have sometimes become individual agents of change, which has discernible effects on their actions. Such a person was Edna Ruth Byler, who was moved by the poverty she saw on a trip to Puerto Rico in 1946 to sell handicrafts imported from Third World artisans in the United States in order to enhance their economic standing. Fifty years later Byler's enterprise became Ten Thousand Villages, a company with about eighty retail stores worldwide that wholesales to hundreds of other stores. Byler's founding of Ten Thousand Villages demonstrates a form of political consumerism in which public action promotes economic justice in a transnational fashion (see www.tenthousandvillages .com and Global Anabaptist Mennonite Encyclopedia Online at www.gameo .org/encyclopedia).

In the 1980s, citizens in the United States and Western Europe concerned with transnational justice formed scores of separate economic and advocacy networks regarding Third World economic products. Such citizens often included participants in religious groups, leftist ideologues worried about the effects of global capitalism, concerned humanists, and, particularly after 1985, American environmentalists whose focus shifted from domestic policy to the recognition that we live on one planet. Public action regarding Third World economic goods, which came to be known as "fair trade," was particularly strong among students and of particular interest to women, political consumerism being a vehicle of participation for the time-limited housewife (Micheletti 2003, 140–144, 157–158).

The idea of fair trade came to mean freedom from the restrictions of the regular market, often itself not "free" but constrained by oligopoly and government regulation. The basic fair-trade idea is to purchase commodities from Third World producers, normally artisans and small farmers under economic stress, who are producing under environmentally sustainable conditions. Such goods are then marketed in high-income nations with a "fair-trade" label, certifying that a fair price was paid to the Third World manufacturers, producing according to environmental sustainability. The fair-trade label assumes some type of mechanism for verifying production conditions: The factory uses no child labor and operates under safe conditions, a product really was made by small farmers working under sustainable conditions, and so forth. The goal is to enhance political consumerism by selling products preferred by citizens concerned with economic justice and the global environment (Micheletti 2003, 94–99; Levi and Linton 2003; Vogel 2005, 100–103).

Regarding fair-trade action around coffee in the United States, a major initiation was the organization of Equal Exchange in 1986 to import coffee from Nicaraguan growers in opposition to an attempted embargo of the Sandinistas by the Reagan administration. In 1988, Max Havelaar, an influential Dutch fair-trade network, was founded to promote fair trade in coffee. (Max Havelaar was a character who opposed colonialism in an 1860 novel.) Also during 1988, American leftists founded Global Exchange to promote fair trade in coffee on a global basis. Founded in 1989, the International Fair Trade Association (IFTA) claimed on its website to have 300 organizations in sixty countries. In 2004, the IFTA organized a certifying process to launch a worldwide trademark for fair-trade organizations, which by 2008 had registered 150 organizations. Indeed the area of fair trade in coffee has become thickly organized; in 2003, Margaret Levi and April Linton listed seventeen separate organizations in the field, counting those that primarily emphasized sustainable agricultural practices in coffee. Thus, in 1996, TransFair U.S. was established as an organization to coordinate the activities of the various coffee fair-trade groups and, in particular, to centralize the certification process for the U.S. use of the fair-trade label for coffee (Levi and Linton 2003, 419–426).

In 2006, Starbucks claimed to be selling 10 percent of the world's fair-trade coffee (www.starbucks.com/aboutus). In 1999, Global Exchange had organized protests in front of Starbucks stores, demanding that it sell fair-trade coffee. At first Starbucks argued that doing so could threaten the quality of its brand, but in 2000 the company agreed and is now the largest retailer of such coffee in the United States. It is unlikely that Starbucks feared a boycott in 2000 would immediately affect its profits, but it had to be concerned about its brand name. Like Nike, Starbucks emerged from the American Northwest in the late 1980s as trendy and "cool," appealing especially to higher-income young professionals with common-good-type concerns. As such Starbucks developed its almost universally recognized logo, the mermaid in the green circle, and had to preserve its image as a green-friendly brand. Starbucks was thus not in a position to put up much resistance to protests by well-organized fair-trade groups; nevertheless, its carrying fair-trade coffee was an important victory for transnational public action (Levi and Linton 2003, 421, 424; Vogel 2005, 104).

Corruption: Transparency International

By its nature political corruption in a first country is not likely to attract widespread anticorruption activism against it within a second country. Unlike questions about the global environment or human rights, the negative chain of events arising from corruption in some country other than that of one's citizenship is not so apparent and is not a priority for citizenship action. Also, in the world of nation-states, action by a group in one country against the political conduct of a group in another tends to violate the norm of national sovereignty and will likely generate wide-scale offense in the country charged with corruption.

However, transnational public action against corruption does exist as an elite phenomenon and actually has some influence. A central element of such action is the transnational group known as Transparency International (TI). The central thread of events leading to the formation of TI grew out of controversies within the World Bank. Around 1990, one faction of World Bank officials argued that corruption within the recipient countries was vitiating the bank's aid program. Development aid does not lead to development if most of it is stolen by corrupt officials. A dissatisfied bank official, Peter Eigen, resigned and spent the next three years building a transnational network of like-minded people regarding political corruption as a top-priority issue, especially within Third World and Eastern European countries. A convention of such people met in Berlin in 1993 and established TI, a group consisting of about seventy delegates from international organizations, multinational corporations, and NGOs. TI was established as an international secretariat to finance and advise local national chapters, each combating corruption within its own country. Seventy national chapters had been established by 1998, while the Berlin secretariat grew rapidly in budget and personnel. TI has close relationships with scores of large businesses, which contribute to national chapters and the international secretariat, and also receives financial support from governments and American foundations.[2]

In 1995, TI established and began to publicize its Corrupt Practices Index (CPI), which soon received worldwide publicity. TI discovered that international marketing has led to the conduct of numerous scattered polls of businesspersons and journalists concerning their perceptions of the degree of corruption practiced within various governments. Such information is valuable to business executives in making investment decisions in one country or another. TI decided to gather, accumulate, and consolidate such polls, giving each country with four or more polls an index number for corruption. For journalists around the world, CPI stories almost write themselves. Furthermore, TI brings out a new CPI index every year, leading to continuing publicity about national corruption. While not likely to have an immediate, direct effect, publicized CPI numbers showing high corruption are an effective issue-framing device for anticorruption politicians and reformers in the more corrupt Third World and post-Communist nations.

The CPI index has an adversarial quality and is issued by the international secretariat in Berlin. However, from its founding, TI has advised its national chapters to work in coalitions with other reformers and, if possible, to develop cooperative arrangements with governmental officials similarly aiming to alleviate corruption. In general, a local chapter would lose influence if viewed as the adversarial agent of an international body. A country chapter may participate in a local advocacy coalition on a rather quiet basis. Rasma Karklins, for instance, reports a case in which the Latvian chapter of TI joined a coalition opposing the construction of an unnecessary sports facility approved after government officials received bribes (2005, 140–141).

The U.S. version of TI is also an elite organization with a Washington, D.C., office, which conducts research funded by about twenty-five corporations and a few foundations. The American branch does not oppose political corruption within the United States, as the TI anticorruption goals are directed toward reform in less-developed and moderately developed countries. TI in the United States gets strong support from domestic business elites because American laws against bribing foreign officials are occasionally enforced, thereby deterring American corporations from engaging in bribery and putting Americans at a disadvantage to foreign competitors whose use of bribery is unchecked by their home countries.

The organization of the TI with its national chapters and CPI index is a case of creative participation and civic innovation, if we take the planet as a frame of reference. People upset about corruption in the Third World are free to contribute to TI on its website, but at least in the United States, few ordinary citizens do so. TI is thus a new form of participation, transnational in nature, but it must be regarded as a form of participation by business leaders and other elites from various nations.

Global Social Forums

In 1999 and 2000, a number of South American and Western European activists devised the idea of having a counterforum to the annual meeting of global economic elites in Davos, Switzerland, known as the World Economic Forum. The leftist city government of Porto Alegre, Brazil, agreed to host such a counterforum, to be known as the World Social Forum (WSF). In January 2001, 8,000 or more participants showed up, including many people from South American countries other than Brazil and a significant number from Europe and the United States. The purpose of the meeting was not to organize demonstrations, at least not directly, but to discuss the issue of a positive platform for activists opposed to a perceived world economic order as represented by the economics ministers and others present at the Davos meeting. As such, organizing the conference might be seen as an act of creative participation on the global level and, in this case, creative participation to create a forum for the discussion of issues regarding the worldwide economy and human rights. In other words, the WSF was one type of participation to create an opportunity for another type of participation, that of public discussion in a forum involving face-to-face interaction.[3]

A major reason behind forming the WSF was to answer the question, What are we for? This question became prominent in the context of the famous 1999 Seattle demonstration against the WTO and subsequent, smaller demonstrations against the IMF and the World Bank, held mostly after the first WSF but declining in significance after 2004. The question of ideology, or perhaps the question of the framing of anticapitalist issues, was not clear in the era after the decline of Marxism, Leninism, Maoism, Fanonism, Catholic liberation theology, the American New Left, the global protests of 1968, nationalist assumption of power in Third World countries, government-planned economies, and "small is beautiful." Many thought free market and international free-trade beliefs, or "neoliberalism," were institutionalized in the WTO, IMF, World Bank, and other international financial institutions, which represented the interests of global, multinational corporations to exploit Third World nations by forcing them to introduce neoliberal financial- and economic-development policies. This served as a core belief attracting WSF participants. However, the question remained as to what new institutions might be established to combat the maldistribution of economic goods seen as perpetuated by neoliberalism.

The idea of the WSF as developed in practice in Porto Alegre in 2001 and 2002 was to organize a large convocation to be broken down into hundreds of specific discussions of particular issues and attended by diverse participants from around the world. The organization was developed by a committee of participating organizations, generally planning yearly meetings for 2001 to 2007. These meetings were held in Porto Alegre in 2001, 2002, and 2003, were moved to Mumbai, India, in 2004, and then went back to Porto Alegre in 2005. Three meetings were held in 2006: in Bamako, Mali; Caracas, Venezuela; and Karachi, Pakistan. The next meeting was held in Nairobi, Kenya, in 2007. After the first meeting in 2001, about 70,000 people showed up to most WSF gatherings, which lasted about a week. However, in 2007 the coordinating body of the WSF decided to suspend the global meetings in favor of regional meetings, such as the European Social Forum, which had previously met in Florence, Paris, London, and Athens. During 2003 to 2006, six regional meetings were held in South America. A major regional meeting for the United States was held in Atlanta in 2007. The WSF council decided to move to regional meetings (at least for a while) to diversify attendance by reducing travel costs for participants, most of whom paid their own way. According to a survey by American academics, 69 percent of the participants in the 2005 Porto Alegre WSF were from South America, and such regional overparticipation likely characterized the other worldwide WSF forums (J. Smith et al. 2008, 52). The WSF brand name is used for local social forums, of which nine were held in the United States from 2002 to 2006 in cities like Boston, New York, Chicago, Houston, Los Angeles, and San Francisco and in the state of Maine (J. Smith et al. 2008, 114).

The 2005 participants at Porto Alegre were 69 percent from South America; 80 percent considered themselves leftists, with 58 percent favoring abolishing capitalism and 42 percent favoring a reform of capitalism. The 2005 survey, supported by surveys taken in 2003 and 2006, found that attendees were younger (42 percent under age twenty-six) and college educated (61 percent with sixteen years of education) (J. Smith et al. 2008, 54). At Porto Alegre, 36 percent were "professionals, technicians, and artists," while 33.3 percent were students. This was not a meeting of the working classes (J. Smith et al. 2008, 55). In terms of movements represented, the 2005 survey found (with some participants listing more than one) 25.2 percent human rights and antiracism, 22.2 percent environmental, 20.8 percent alternative media and culture, 18.8 percent global justice,

17.7 percent peace, 13.6 percent socialism, 11.3 percent labor, 10.5 percent fair trade, 10.3 percent women's rights, and eight others getting significant listing (J. Smith et al. 2008, 63).

The WSF was largely a South American and European movement. Only 10 percent or less of the attendees were from the United States, even though most of the participants at the 1999 Seattle demonstration were Americans (J. Smith et al. 2008, 52). Probably one reason for such unexpectedly low American participation in the WSF was U.S. activists' primary concern with protesting the Iraq War during this period (Hadden and Tarrow 2007).

The number of individual participants in global, regional, and local WSF events has apparently been on the order of 1 million. Broken down into several thousand separate discussion groups, the aggregate of WSF participation is certainly significant, at least in terms of forum participation and individual development of political ideas. Given the overrepresentation of South Americans, the WSF likely had its greatest impact on activists from that area. The WSF did not define itself as a body issuing a platform for its constituents, but a subgroup at the Bamako, Mali, WSF in 2006 did list twelve reasonably specific types of objectives, including cancelling Third World debt, taxing international financial transactions, eliminating international tax-free havens, establishing the right to work as a worldwide human right, promoting international fair trade (not free trade), eliminating agricultural subsidies in developed nations, prohibiting patents on living organisms and private ownership of water, developing environmental sustainability and preventing global warming, opposing various types of discrimination for indigenous people, reforming and democratizing international organizations, eliminating foreign military bases, and promulgating a human right to information not controlled by governments or media conglomerates. Thus, the WSF has been a body to frame issues (J. Smith et al. 2008, 141–145) and may have already reached its height with the participation of 155,000 people at the 2005 Porto Alegre WSF (J. Smith et al. 2008, 58).

Conclusion

This chapter indicates that there is quite a variety of modes of transnational political participation, usually reflected in advocacy networks, as exemplified by the Nestlé boycott, the Brent Spar uproar, the politics of shopping for clothing and shoes from the Third World, fair-trade consumerism for coffee and other products, support for Transparency International, and the creation of global social forums. Globalization is clearly a massive social force that increases many citizens' desire to participate in the shaping of events outside their homeland. The trend of global participation is likely to accelerate in the early decades of the twenty-first century.

People want to participate in the politics of a country even though they are not its citizens. The formation of transnational advocacy networks is public action only secondarily related to traditional forms of political participation within the home country, such via established political institutions, civic engagement, or social movements. The desire for transnational participation has led to creative participation by individuals through the formation of new advocacy networks to influence the politics of countries other their own.

Notes

1. Jordan 2001 is the major source for this section.

2. The material in this section is largely based upon Galtung and Pope 1999; Kuper 2004; the Transparency International and Transparency International–USA websites at www.transparency.org and www.transparency-usa.org, respectively, and Transparency International's *Annual Report* 2007.

3. The material in this section is largely based on della Porta 2007, chs. 1, 10; Pianta and Marchetti 2007; Hadden and Tarrow 2007; J. Smith et al. 2008.

CHAPTER 7

CONCLUSION

CREATIVE PARTICIPATION IN THE TWENTY-FIRST CENTURY

A central goal of this book is to show that several different concepts of political participation exist. This variety is analogous to the variety of concepts of representation demonstrated by political philosopher Hanna Fenichel Pitkin and now accepted by the various branches of political science. As with political representation, so it is with political participation. Indeed, political scientists normally recognize that there are different concepts of participation, but such recognition is stated unclearly and in the form of partial statements. For instance, it is conventional to contrast the idea of participation as being part of a debate about community issues with one expressing one's interests within a system of political institutions. And it is also the conventional understanding that discussions of participation as civic engagement differ from discussions of participation as voting and contributing to an interest group. However, others have not identified the five forms of participation as I have in this book.

Political scientists are familiar with the four types of political participation identified as the forum, interests and institutions, civic engagement, and political movements. Therefore, it was not my priority in this book to write a chapter about each of the four with numerous citations to the literature, as Pitkin did in her work on representation. Such a task may fall to some other writer, who likely may have some partial objection to my list of five types of participation.

Instead, I have emphasized the idea of creative participation as civic innovation, a fifth concept of political participation that has not been identified in the literature. This springs from the observation that there are circumstances in which considerable numbers of scattered individuals lack an established institutional mode to pursue public action to achieve some commonweal goal (a common good). At times such scattered individuals devise new modes of political participation. They engage in creative political participation for some civic innovation. This often involves new techniques, such as uses of the Internet. Indeed, the term "creative participation" might be an ordinary language usage for Internet political participation, such as uses of e-mail, Facebook, meet-ups, and so forth. However, in this book I normally use creative participation in the more restrictive sense of the fifth type of participation.

The idea of creative political participation is tied to the paradoxes of participation. There are instances of political action in which joint action seems impossible, fruitless, or not sustainable, even though the goals of such joint action are vital to the community. By now social science is familiar with Mancur Olson Jr.'s logic of collective action in which the few defeat the many because the many lack incentives to mobilize and maintain organizations to achieve the public goods they seek. Political scientists are generally familiar with Garrett Hardin's tragedy of the commons, formulated by Elinor Ostrom as the dilemma of common-pool resources, in which individuals have the incentive to rush to deplete them rather than to organize together to sustain the common pool. Often citizens are caught in the famous situation of the prisoner's dilemma, in which problems of communication prevent joint action to achieve the commonweal. Instances of creative political participation cited in this book are means by which individuals overcome these paradoxes of political participation.

Creative participation at the mass level includes contributions to environmental lobbies in the United States, the recycling of household throwaways, tens of thousands of local protests by rural Chinese, cross-class activity by Wisconsin town dwellers against corruption in the 1890s, demonstrations in the capitals of countries undergoing "color revolutions," the reaction against Shell Oil in the Brent Spar incident, Internet-coordinated protests against ExxonMobil as a reaction against corporate power, boycotts against Nestlé and various clothing manufacturers contracting with Asian factories, and global social forums. Examples of creative participation by elites include participation in transnational advocacy networks, environmental lobbying at headquarters in Washington, D.C., and publicity campaigns against corruption by Transparency International.

From the standpoint of political issue areas, environmental issues commonly provide contexts for creative participation. Environmental issues have been often characterized as issues appealing to numerous, scattered citizens, lacking established political institutions to provide means for public action. Accordingly, public-interest lobbies and transnational advocacy networks have been created to pursue the attainment of environmental public goods. Almost by definition, political-corruption issues provide contexts for creative participation because, in this area, the established political institutions are the target for reform, if only the scattered reformers can create new modes of public participation. Political consumers sometimes act directly against a large business corporation or other producer in the economic market. At the national or transnational levels, consumer boycotts might initially seem to be hopeless, but effective publicity for a boycott can erode the economic worth of a brand name and accompanying corporate logo, thereby giving political consumers leverage.

Established political institutions in one nation frequently appear ineffective in influencing the public policies of other countries. In this case, creative political participation leads to the formation of transnational advocacy networks that may act in the politics of the second country. The advocacy network may be mobilized into an interest group in the first country with the hope of lobbying its national parliament to take foreign policy actions against the second country, resulting in the so-called boomerang effect.

But why then should creative participation be seen as one of a series of different concepts of political participation? A first reason is the simple academic reason. Since there is such a series of different concepts, scholars should be aware of this while doing their work. But to move beyond this, the five concepts provide a context for each singular concept in conducting scholarship. An important example is the relationship between the now preeminent civic-engagement concept and the creative-participation concept (see Chapter 1). The publications of leading civic-engagement scholars such as Robert Putnam and Theda Skocpol leave one confused as to their ideas about the role of public-interest lobbies, transnational advocacy networks, political consumerism, and other such modes of political participation. These do not involve civic engagement, but how do they fit in to the authors' overall views about political participation? Putnam refers to individuals as contributors to, but not "members" of, such groups. Skocpol paints a negative picture of elite Washington lobbies, directed by professional organizers and lobbyists, without much tie to a membership (see Chapters 1 and 2). It would advance the discussion to recognize that public-interest lobbies play an important role in dealing with the paradoxes of participation, even while civic engagement enhances social trust. The political reality of representation here is one of two different modes of participation.

Creative participation enriches the discussion of politics by dealing with questions arising from the paradoxes of participation. In the forum, everyone is together and communicating. There is no such paradox. In the framework of interests and institutions, Olson's logic of collective action leads to an observation that the few defeat the many, probably in most public-policy areas. But this does not happen so often, at least not so simply, and we need to turn to the creative participation of forming citizens lobbies to understand the reality of political representation. As noted, almost by definition, the theory of civic engagement excludes the paradoxes of participation because civic engagement is based on the idea of face-to-face interaction as leading to the formation of the social capital of trust. Political-movement participation is more similar to creative participation in that new forms of political and social action are created by movement participants. However, political movements normally seek to redefine the identity of participants and to advance the welfare of some particular group, unlike creative participation in its search for the commonweal.

Two or more forms of participation may be linked in a time sequence. During the years from 1970 to 1974, it was creative participation to form a Washington lobby to further environmental or clean-government legislation. Subsequently, however, such commonweal lobbying became institutionalized so that people with public-interest concerns would know automatically how to send in a check. Creative participation gave way to a form of interests-and-institutions participation. Or protests against contamination of local water supplies might bring together scattered citizens within the local community, who might then continue to associate in a face-to-face manner, developing social trust—hence the social capital of civic engagement. Or the causal processes can go from political movements toward creative participation. For instance, the political movement of environmentalism can influence scattered citizens to engage in recycling, a form of creative participation. Or the previous educational efforts of the environmental movement might make northern Europeans sensitive to the idea of a multinational corporation's polluting the North Sea, leading to political consumerist protest against oil companies.

In the case of environmentalism, it seems that political-movement and creative participation overlap because environmentalism is a commonweal movement, unlike many other political movements. Some activists may be basically movement oriented regarding the environment, in Alberto Melucci's (1996) sense of a political movement as embodying "critical codes" in relation to existing institutions. Environmentalists advocating major changes in political and legal institutions thus advocate a critical code and engage in political-movement participation. This would differ from those engaging in creative participation, such as advocating recycling, or the political consumerism of buying local food for the sake of the environment. Observers of environmental activism would find the two forms of participation coexisting, while a particular individual might move from one to another as, for instance, creative political participation may be radicalized into movement militancy.

Balanced Participation

Balanced participation is a very important idea for the understanding of political participation in a democracy. I find that there are five different types of participation; others might argue for a different number. But the exact number may not matter that much. It is important for democratic government that none of the five types of participation be seen in isolation from the others.

For democracy it is important that none of the types be exaggerated beyond a due proportion. Democracy is not all political discussion in the forum. Nor is it all the expression of interests to be represented in a system of institutions. Nor is democracy just civic engagement, trust, and the formation of social capital or just the development and expression of social and political identity in movements. Nor is it just creative participation as scattered individuals create new modes of public action. Democracy requires each of these five forms of political participation.

Further, democracy is enhanced when the different types of political participation are balanced. The concepts of the political forum and expressing interests through institutions were briefly separated until, following the initiation of the discussion known as the theory of "deliberative democracy," political scientists saw that these two modes needed to be related and joined (Fishkin 1992). It is not democracy if interests are expressed but never discussed; nor is it wise to theorize about democracy as if everyone lived today in city-states resembling ancient Athens. The two concepts of the forum and institutional representation of interests must be seen in some mode of balance. Similarly one should not separate the political participation concepts of civic engagement and expression of interests in institutions. As the best treatments of civic engagement recognize, face-to-face interaction at the level of neighborhoods and communities usually does build trust and social capital, which is a foundation for the act of voting and for the mobilization and maintenance of interest groups. Again the two concepts of participation must be seen as acting in balance for the appropriate enhancement of democracy.

Balanced participation is important for democracy as we view the relationship of creative participation to the other concepts. The creative participation of the first stages of expressing an environmental concern will give way to the institutional stage of the Washington lobby, entailing bureaucracy, professional management, and "politics as usual"(Bosso 2005). On the other hand, the Washington lobby should continue to act in balance with forms of creative participation as partial insurance against neglecting its public interests for the sake of organizational interests. The civic-engagement perspective must be balanced with the recognition of the very strong demands of the logic of collective action. Scattered individuals desiring some commonweal goal must in some sense get together to start to develop social trust among themselves, and finding the means to get together is a form of creative participation. First there must be creative participation, then civic engagement, then institutional expression of some commonweal goal (interest).

A very important participatory balance is that required to enhance democracy in the implementation of public policy. One must not forget that after a law has been debated, possibly supported by a political movement and by groups dependent on social capital, and after legislation has been enacted through the processes of representation of interests in institutions, the law and its public policy must be implemented and effectively implemented over a succeeding period of perhaps a decade. As a great amount of research indicates, public attention and debate, as well as the political movement supporting many laws, wane after enactment. Accordingly, and as specified by Olson's emphasis on the few defeating the many by the organization of political oligopolies to reinterpret a public policy according to their own agendas, the intentions of the original legislators may be undermined by the well-organized influence of a group acting for its own interests. This is a well-known problem of policy implementation that can often be countered by creative participation, as when Chinese rural dwellers rush to protest local corruption or Progressive Midwesterners created new forms of public action against the corruption of local utility contracting. In the field of American national environmental policy and regulation, creative participation has led to the formation of effective watchdog lobbies to prevent regulation from being redefined and limited in the interests of those to be regulated. While face-to-face participation in local civic-engagement processes is an important form of political participation, such local engagement cannot produce the type of political participation necessary to monitor and influence environmental implementation policy, often highly technical in nature. Political participation must be balanced to enable effective and fair implementation of environmental laws.

This is not to say that creative participation is always a good thing or that it always enhances democracy. Many readers would conclude that the Dixie Chicks boycott in support of President George W. Bush did not enhance the commonweal by, in this case, arguing that the office of U.S. president must be respected by not criticizing its current holder outside U.S. borders. Some anti-immigration advocates may join vigilante groups out of a sincere belief that immigration policy must be fairly implemented in the face of the efforts of economic special interests who hire immigrants at low wages, thereby undermining laws designed to express a commonweal interests such as control of the borders, public health, and public safety.

Creative Participation and Worldwide Social Change

As we move deeper into the twenty-first century, we will likely see more of creative participation as a response to worldwide social change. Despite its overuse, the term "globalization" is still useful in directing attention to the increasing frequency and necessity of using a worldwide frame of reference for political action. Issues have become more and more planetary, going beyond the framework of the nation-state. This is especially true of environmental issues, which almost by definition eventually surpass the local and wind up with a planetary frame of reference, as our final environment is, of course, the planet Earth as a whole. Creative political participation is particularly oriented to the paradoxes of political action in the situation of common-pool resources and the need for political participation to cooperate to preserve such commonweal resources. Issues such as global warming, the preservation of ocean environments including fish and fisheries, the relationship of local forests to the overall planetary environment, and the use of limited natural resources, such as petroleum, fresh water, or various minerals, have become global. In terms of global issues, political action naturally transcends state boundaries, calling for the formation of transnational advocacy networks as a creative participatory response of scattered individuals concerned with the commonweal of the planet. Or within the boundaries of democratic or even semiauthoritarian states, creative participation occurs as citizens use new technologies to forge environmental associations and lobbies to influence their own governments.

Creative participation is not only manifested in global political action but also forms a part of local political action. In itself, the creative participation of 700 million Chinese rural villagers is public action by 12 percent of the planet's population. As noted, rural Chinese act in tens of thousands of recorded protests per year against corrupt local officials manipulating land sales, desecrating the environment, directly or indirectly stealing public funds, and manipulating local village elections. This is not exactly social-movement participation because the protestors accept the status quo of political authority in China and seek to apply the status quo of legality to their local village. One might go beyond this 12 percent of humanity and look for similar local creative participation in other places. Such examples can be found in rural and small-town protests against corruption against the backdrop of modern manufacturing and infrastructure development. As another example, small farmers in India have acted to block the construction of a major automobile factory, whose owners have a kind of eminent domain authority to preempt ownership of farmland. We may tend to sympathize with the economics of modernization, but creative participation includes local resistance to changes in land control imposed by authorities seeking economic development (Sengupta 2008).

Creative participation is manifested locally in environmental actions. Such action is not limited to uncoordinated, environmentally oriented decisions by individuals, such as the decision to recycle. Both in rural China and in Woburn, Massachusetts, local residents have formed new mechanisms of public action to combat environmental degradation, including unsafe pollution, in their neighborhoods. The so-called negative externalities (effects) of manufacturing enterprises and infrastructural construction projects occur daily in thousands of places around the world. We can thus expect numerous examples of creative participation by people seeking to restore the commonweal good of an uncorrupted environment in their localities. Locally oriented creative participation for the environment may be one of the more striking political phenomena of the twenty-first century.

In the capital square phenomenon, creative participation melds the local and the national—as when creative participation in a "color" revolution is automatically coordinated and expressed in the geographical layout of a capital city. I witnessed a more local form of protest in 2008 in Oaxaca, Mexico, where a score of leftist and indigenous groups protested the state governor by establishing a multiyear encampment of about 1,000 people in the central square.

Many strands of creative participation can be woven into public action during the policy-implementation stage of the governing process. Pollyannaish civics teachers and lawyers fixed on categories may suppose that politics ends with legislative decisions, but those concerned with the effects of public policy—citizens, businesspersons, interest-group employees, lobbyists—know that the passage of a law is not the end of the process. Laws can be partially, or even wholly, reversed during the policy-implementation process. Special interests can continually press for change when they are no longer opposed by reformist morning glories (open in the morning but closed in the afternoon) in the image of Boss G. W. Plunkitt of Tammany Hall. Local-level creative participation against environmental degradation is often a protest against the lack of implementation of environmental laws, whether in Szechuan or Massachusetts. A major goal of the formation of environmental lobbies in the United States is to see to the continued enforcement of environmental laws and regulations, which may not be enforced by politicians who avoid interference in the marketplace, simply favor increased corporate profits, or are courting those who make campaign contributions. I would now characterize the formation of environmental lobbies as an instance of balanced participation, with the original act of organization entailing creative participation; as such lobbies become established, they become another instance of the institutionalization of interests, although the interests represented are purportedly for the common good rather than special interests.

Certainly the formation of analogous groups in countries other than the United States will likely become a common form of political participation, and like such groups in the United States, environmental groups elsewhere will become institutionalized and participate in the policy process in their own arenas, even in authoritarian systems such as that of China. We do have evidence that the formation of transnational environmental advocacy networks, a somewhat different phenomenon from public-interest groups, has burgeoned during the last generation (Keck and Sikkink 1998, ch. 1).

New Technologies

The new technologies of the Internet and cell phones are becoming very much a part of creative participation. This is not to say that the use of new technologies is limited to creative participation: Blogging is a new type of forum participation; Internet fund-raising is having a major impact on American electoral finances; civic-engagement groups such as parent-teacher associations can coordinate activities by establishing Facebook networks. However, creative participation by definition involves the creation of new modes of political participation by previously scattered individuals who lack established institutions to pursue commonweal goals. The Internet, by its very nature, is a technology that brings together scattered individuals, that is, those who lack the face-to-face interaction of civic engagement or activity within established institutions. For the most part, we can regard scattering as referring to geographically separated individuals who do not see one another and, for the most part, do not even know about each other (although they assume unknown others share their common-good goals). However, a scattering need not refer only to individuals. Thus, a scattering may at once include geographically separate individuals, interactive social networks, and even organized groups. Creative participation occurs as individuals and perhaps representatives of social networks and organized groups somehow communicate, possibly then meeting, to form a vehicle for political action.

A striking case of the links between creative participation and Internet use occurred in the Iranian anticorruption protests concerning that country's June 2009 election. Almost every press account regarding the initial mass protests stressed the significance of Twitter, Facebook, YouTube, and various forms of Internet communication to inform supporters of Mir-Hossein Moussavi about the flow of events in various places and to include information about the time and place of ongoing mass demonstrations. Individuals outside of Iran joined the Iranian protest activity on the Internet; similarly, software developed by Falun Gong, the Chinese exercising religion, was given to the protestors to elude server shutdowns and other Internet-control measures (Kristof 2009). The U.S. State Department actually requested that Twitter delay a scheduled maintenance shutdown for the area including Iran (Landler and Stelter 2009).

This book provides examples of creative participation preceding the widespread use of the Internet, but many of these participatory actions are likely to flourish even more in the present and future world of online ubiquity. In particular, Internet-coordinated protest groups have formed in relation to certain multinational corporations, such as ExxonMobil and Shell Oil, and while often dormant and only marginally effective, they can serve as core communication units to spread information about protest as major new issues arise in relation to global warming, relations to indigenous people, environmental scandals, and so forth. In the area of political consumerism, Internet communication can facilitate boycotting or preferential buying behavior, as individuals on e-mail networks and Facebook learn about the formulation of action through the Internet. Authoritarian governments such as those in Iran or China can fight back against the new technologies by the direct means of shutting down servers or blocking numerous websites. However, multinational corporations do not have these powers and, thus, may find themselves continually subject to influence exercised by Internet protestors.

The anti–Dixie Chicks protest developed out of new technology. It originated with Internet networks of country music fans spreading Natalie Maines's statement that condemned President G. W. Bush. Within twenty-four hours, right-wing, patriotic Internet networks picked up this information and promulgated the idea of boycotting the Chicks. The original report was a review in the traditional medium of a newspaper, but within a few days it had spread to hundreds of thousands of Internet users as interpreted within the frame of speaking disloyally about the president in a foreign country. It then affected the playlists of country music radio stations and subsequent CD sales, both older technologies. This example reminds us that new technologies in creative participation can be used by citizens with traditional views about political authority, as well as by "cool" technologists rebelling against tradition.

It is important to realize that Internet technology does not simply create new local networks and bring them into politics to act by themselves. A key technological step in present and future politics is whether locally created Internet networks will manage to federalize themselves throughout the nation-state. For instance, in tens of thousands of Chinese rural villages, local protest networks can form on the Internet to communicate about local corruption in a single village of perhaps 1,000 people. This would not be highly threatening to the Communist regime, especially if almost all of these local Internet networks spread information about laws of the national regime and urged all parties to follow them. However, to the extent that hundreds or even thousands of local protest networks link with one another, the potential for sudden criticism of the regime's overall national policies becomes apparent. A similar situation could occur in Iran if local Facebook groups and Twitter users moved toward federalizing into a nationwide network, informing one another of regime blunders and resulting local protests. New frameworks of political interpretation and calls for public action can then circulate if there is a national communications flow among hundreds of local networks. However, authoritarian national governments will strive to prevent such nationwide linkages among local networks, resulting in a contest of communications strategies as authorities try to block Internet usage while reformers work up new modes of evading the blockades, normally with the assistance of foreign computer experts.

Widely dispersed new types of visual technology are having a significant impact upon politics, including creative participation. By now we are familiar with images recorded by portable video cameras later circulating on television and, more recently, on YouTube. The video recording of three Los Angeles police officers beating Rodney King in 1991 precipitated a huge political controversy, and even a major riot, and may be remembered as a landmark event illustrating the political impact of new video technology. Surreptitious videos taken by animal rights activists in breeding factories and slaughterhouses were later shown to millions of people. With the emergence of YouTube, it became possible for Iranian protestors to circulate videos of demonstrators being beaten in Teheran in almost real time. In 2010, the full impact of YouTube technology on politics has yet to become apparent.

Internet technology obviously has a significant potential for enhancing the organization of international advocacy networks as forms of creative participation. However, I am not in a position to make definitive statements, and we must await the systematic collection of data about the use of new technologies in transnational organizing. Yet I can point to specific types of examples.

We need to take more seriously the Falun Gong (exercise religion) movement in China and its activities after being forced into oppositional politics by the persecution of the Beijing regime, perhaps out of fear of a recreation of the huge, religion-based, nineteenth-century Taiping rebellion. To my surprise, it seems that Falun Gong adherents are world leaders in the technology of hiding the source of Internet messages, apparently relying on a global Internet network based in China and the United States. This same group gave Internet-security advice to the Iranian protestors in June 2009.

Unpublished research by University of Illinois, Chicago, graduate student Herman Maiba indicated that transnational committees of Internet coordinators played a key role in organizing at least some of the international protests between 1999 and 2005 against international organizations and governments alleged to be forcing neoliberal policies on Third World nations (e.g., world trade undermining indigenous economies). While now apparently in decline, such demonstrations with international support in Seattle, Genoa, Barcelona, and elsewhere attained worldwide attention. As noted, new Internet technology seems to be a necessary condition for the organization of watchdog groups, each focused on the activities of a single multinational corporation.

A visit to the Greenpeace and Amnesty International websites indicates the usefulness of the Internet in communicating a transnational advocacy network's activities to its international constituency and at least serving as a means for increasing contributions. Amnesty International has its own network on Facebook and posts its own blog; I take its activities to be typical of many groups expressing themselves on the Internet. Similarly, parallel groups in different countries, such as those in Britain and the United States protesting the use of baby formula and promoting breast feeding, can read one another's websites for new ideas while raising one another's morale and demonstrating that their cause is truly global.

Straightforward uses of the simple cell phone should not be neglected in a discussion of new technologies and creative participation. Reports indicate that the cell phone was important in organizing the Orange Revolution in the Ukraine (McFaul 2005, 12), which focused on mass demonstrations in the government square in Kiev. Cell phones are clearly useful in organizing and directing demonstrations, cancelling out the advantage of police use of shortwave radio, which demonstrators have used less frequently during the last generation. In the United States, at least, protest demonstrations have often been coordinated by a leadership group using electrically enhanced megaphones, or microphones and amps, which may not be effective tools for coordinating very large demonstrations, for giving route directions during marches, or for communicating sudden changes in activity by police or counterdemonstrators. Demonstrations can usually be broken down into subnetworks of participating groups or simply into networks of friends and neighbors demonstrating together (Danaher and Burbach 2000; Rucht, Teune and Yang 2007). It improves the coherence and morale of a demonstration if such subgroups can readily form and communicate with one another, which is much more feasible in a world in which everyone possesses a cell phone.

The technological revolution of the Internet should not mask our observation of the introduction of technologies into creative participation and social movements in earlier times, even though with the Internet, references to such earlier technologies now seems mundane. For instance, the Brent Spar protest as described in Grant Jordan's book largely occurred as the result of television news broadcasts of images of Greenpeace protestors being attacked with fire hoses. Television images of dogs attacking peaceful protestors on the bridge in Selma,

Alabama, did much to enhance the Dr. Martin Luther King Jr.'s civil rights movement. Television images of the Santa Barbara oil spill and the *Exxon Valdez* tanker disaster in Alaska strengthened the environmental movement. Such visual images have a greater effect on audiences than sound portrayals on radio.

The introduction of early computer coordination and labeling from potential contributor lists greatly aided mass-mailing techniques in organizing public-interest groups in the early 1970s. The introduction of long-distance telephone service, and its enhancement and much lower cost after 1960, is another technology that aided creative participation and other forms of political activity (McFarland 1976, 21–22; McFarland 1984, 31–32). Both technological and political change surely stretch way back into history; consider the numerous effects of the invention of the printing press. The Internet surely is revolutionary and will produce major changes in political organization. Many will occur in elections, lobbying, civic engagement, and other familiar forms of political activity, but Internet-induced change will play a special role in creative participation due to the medium's merging of scattered individuals and networks to take coherent public action.

Twenty-First Century Practices and Behavior

The earthshaking social trends of the times sometimes generate creative participation. Meeting the challenges of planetary environmental degradation calls forth transnational advocacy networks. Preservation of common-pool resources, such as the riches and purity of the oceans, also elicits citizen participation. The new need for national and planetary energy policy affects citizens concerned with cost, conservation, and ecological responsibility. Political corruption has always been with us, but new and challenging modes of special-interest privateering develop with the increasing complexity of technology and government regulation. Capitalist corporations grow larger and more complex, transcending national borders and creating irritation, frustration, and an ethical sense of responsibility for workers and consumers across the globe. Such issues of social change and political policy exist not only at the level of planetwide action but also at the levels of national, local, and even individual action, such as household recycling.

Creative participation around the world is likely to flourish as citizens act to meet such challenges. This form of participation thus deserves study and discussion—not dismissal as lacking in civic engagement or sometimes leading only to action by educated activists skilled in technology. Yet, I do not expect creative participation to replace civic engagement or standard participation in institutions such as elections or interest groups. Research and discussion will show how creative participation is linked to the other four forms of participation in a balanced manner.

Let us be more specific about the practices and behavior that will flourish in the twenty-first century due to the planetwide challenges and other issues just cited. First, throughout the world in nations allowing latitude for citizens to petition government, *public-interest groups* will become more numerous. This will occur through a parallel mechanism to events in the United States around 1970: Scattered citizens desiring public action to achieve some commonweal goal will work with resource mobilizers to form an organization to influence elites. Governments have become larger, more complex, and more embedded with technology. Policy implementation remains a centerpiece of governance in every country. Because of the logic of collective action, ordinary citizens have difficulty influencing the policy-implementation process. Such frustrated citizens are likely to form public-interest groups to organize and maintain citizen interests during the policy-implementation process.

In addition to citizen action on domestic policies and their implementation, *transnational advocacy networks* will expand and become more numerous as citizens worldwide seek modes by which they can personally act to protest and influence public policies within nations other than their own. An increase in transnational advocacy groups actually has been apparent since 1985, while since 1995 use of the Internet has made them much easier to mobilize and maintain. One interesting possibility is that there could be an increase in transnational action to combat corruption, as the world discovers that corrupt governments in their local policies undermine worldwide action on environmental issues, such as reducing carbon emissions. A planetwide civil society is developing from transnational citizens groups and their advocacy networks, a significant phenomenon but one that we should not overplay as some kind of trend toward world federalism.

Protests, uprisings, and creative participation in rural China occur within a demographic of 700 million people, 12 percent of the population of the planet, a population greater than that of Latin America. As such *Chinese rural protest* deserves major attention from the standpoint of political participation and public action. In this case, perhaps public policies from the Chinese center will substantially decrease the number of protests by the year 2030. New modes of public participation will probably develop in China to express in more institutionalized fashion the civic aims of Chinese rural residents.

As the Chinese example illustrates, creative participation may be local and need not be aimed directly at global issues. Accordingly, throughout the world, creative participation exists on an individual level in the daily practices of citizens, many of whom might be seen as average, "everyday" people. In particular, creative participation is manifested in individual household efforts at recycling. Such "everyday-makers" in the millions come to restrain energy usage and their consumption of consumer items in the interest of conserving common-pool resources, such as water and forests.

Creative participation will continue to find expression in behavior and practice as political consumerism. Of particular interest is transnational political consumerism in an era of continuing economic globalism and the multinational corporation, such as Nestlé or ExxonMobil. Entities of international capitalism will increasingly affect people's lives, and they will occasionally protest directly to the offending corporation or organization. In other cases, numerous scattered citizens will conclude that they should assume responsibility for the ethical treatment of foreign workers and foreign environmental conditions by their own corporations. At times, protest to existing transnational organizations or one's domestic government will seem unsatisfactory—as unlikely to have an effective result—leading to political consumerism.

The frequency of consumerist action will likely increase because of the possibilities of coordinating through Internet technology the desire for public action by scattered citizens. This is especially true in the case of transnational political consumerism. Of course, political consumerism need not be transnational but may be directed at a domestic corporation or other economic actors, including media celebrities. In any case, the corporate logo has become an increasingly important form of symbolic expression and presents an inviting target for consumer protest, stimulating increased support for political consumerist activity. Indeed, coordinated through the Internet, apparently long-lasting protest networks have mobilized and directed themselves against specific corporations, such as Walmart, ExxonMobil, and Nestlé.

A Neo-Progressive Era?

I speculate here that American politics is moving into a new era, a neo-Progressive era, and that creative participation will be a part of this. We may observe politics becoming more oriented toward public-interest protest and regulating business, in a fashion similar to the changes in American politics following the end of the Gilded Age and beginning around the time of Teddy Roosevelt's accession to the presidency. This period, often dated 1901 to 1914 and usually described as an era of progressive reform in American politics, is symbolized by the domestic actions of Presidents Theodore Roosevelt and Woodrow Wilson. This was a time when the untrammeled power of monopolistic corporations and urban political machines met with successful challenges by Progressive reformers, who tended to hail from the rising strata of the new professionals of the middle class (Wiebe 1967), though sometimes Progressive coalitions were communitywide, as noted by David Thelen (see Chapter 3 above). The politics of the Progressive era revolved around the pursuit of the "public interest" against the "special interests" as represented by corporate monopolies and urban patronage machines. Robert Putnam, the chief theorist of civic engagement, actually calls for a return to Progressive politics in the last chapter of *Bowling Alone*. In fact, this may actually happen, with creative participation forming part of such a new political era.

We note that a neo-Progressive era is not so similar to Franklin Delano Roosevelt's New Deal—a coalition of local political-party groups, unions, and liberals—working to stabilize the economy, redistribute income, and provide the basis for a limited welfare state. Nor is neo-progressivism so similar to the identity, antiwar, and lifestyle movements of the 1960s. There is an overlap, however, in the environmental movement, which got a new start around 1968.

A neo-Progressive political era would likely incorporate the goals of environmentalism and conservation of common-pool resources, opposition to political and corporate corruption, and concern for the implementation of public policies to render them more than symbolic. The earlier Progressives were particularly concerned with the implementation of public policies; however, overly impressed with the new scientific professionalism, they overemphasized the possibilities for effective implementation by apolitical, independent regulatory commissions (Bernstein 1955). Like Teddy Roosevelt, neo-Progressives will be more ready to regulate business. Like Woodrow Wilson, they will be concerned with democracy and human rights in foreign nations. The neo-Progressives will constantly affirm that they represent the public interest and are the true opponents of the special interests.

They have this affirmation in common with Progressives and creative participationists. All see themselves as opposing political and economic corruption, as representing the consumer against the excesses of corporate profit taking, and as protecting the environment and common-pool resources against the shortsighted actions of the special interests. The original Progressives looked to scientific regulatory agencies to shepherd the implementation of public policy; the new creative participationists look to the more political actions of public-interest lobbies wielding countervailing power to special-interest iron triangles. The Progressives, neo-Progressives, and creative participationists tend to be led by technically sophisticated, middle-class professionals (Wiebe 1967; Skocpol 2004).

Creative participation may be a factor characteristic of a neo-Progressive political era, while neo-Progressive norms and ideals will induce further creative participation. This does not mean that creative participation will be a dominant political characteristic of a new political era. However, creative participation may become a more important political phenomenon than it is now. The politics of interests and institutions will continue to carry more weight than creative participation, which lends itself to eventual institutionalization into continuing public-interest lobbies. Creative participation may partially replace civic engagement as the widespread use of Internet coordination replaces face-to-face interaction in neighborhoods.

Thus, creative participation and its use of the Internet will become a more important political characteristic in protests against environmental pollution, depletion of common-pool resources, political corruption, inept corporate policies, and the desire to be politically active across national borders. To a great degree, creative participation is now bound up with the use and development of Internet technology.

The phrase "creative participation" has a positive ring in its reference to the efforts of scattered citizens to create new forms of public action when established forms seem not to provide a means to pursue commonweal goals. For the sake of balance, I note that some observers will object to the actions and goals of some such participatory activists, as some would object to casting idealistic opponents of immigration into a positive light.

On the whole, those engaging in creative participation strive to deal with paradoxes of human cooperation that might place severe limits on democracy. Those active in creative participation normally assume personal responsibility for improving society and the welfare of others, not just themselves. As such creative participation is a form of ethical conduct that serves as a basis for ethical citizenship.

Bibliography

Ackelsberg, Martha. 2003. Broadening the study of women's participation. In *Women and American politics*, ed. Susan Carroll, 214–236. New York: Oxford University Press.

Adam, Daniel. 2006. Royal Society tells Exxon: Stop funding climate change denial. *Guardian*. September 20. www.guardian.co.uk/environment/2006/sep/20/oilandpetrol.business (accessed January 23, 2010).

Andersen, Jorgen Goul, and Mette Tobiasen. 2001. Political consumption and political consumers: Globalization and political consumption in the daily life. Working paper, Aarhus University, Institute of Political Science, English translation.

———. 2004. Who are these political consumers anyway? Survey evidence from Denmark. In *Politics, products, and markets*, eds. Michele Micheletti, Andreas Follesdal, and Dietlind Stolle, 203–222. New Brunswick, NJ: Transaction Publishers.

Arendt, Hannah. 1998. *The human condition*. 2nd ed. Chicago: University of Chicago Press.

Associated Press. 2003. Radio consolidation could hurt free expression, senators say. First Amendment Center. July 9. www.firstamendmentcenter.org/news.aspx?id=11694 (accessed January 23, 2010).

Axelrod, Robert. 2006. *The evolution of cooperation*. Rev. ed. New York: Perseus Books.

Bachrach, Peter J. 1967. *The theory of democratic elitism: A critique*. Boston: Little, Brown.

Bang, Henrik. 2003. *Governance as social and political communication*. Manchester, UK: University of Manchester Press.

Barnes, Samuel, and Max Kaase. 1979. *Political action: Mass participation in five Western democracies*. Beverly Hills, CA: Sage Press.

Barringer, Felicity. 2005. Exxon Mobil becomes focus of a boycott. *New York Times*. July 12. www.nytimes.com/2005/07/12/politics/12exxon.html?-r=1 (accessed January 23, 2010).

BBC News. 2003. Dixies dropped over Bush remark. BBC News. March 20. http:// news.bbc.co.uk/1/hi/entertainment/music/2867221.stm (accessed January 23, 2010).

Beck, Ulrich. 1999. *World risk society.* Cambridge, UK: Polity Press.

———. 2000. *What is globalization?* Cambridge, UK: Polity Press.

Bennett, W. Lance. 1998. The uncivic culture: Communication, identity, and the rise of lifestyle politics. *Political Science and Politics* 31, no. 4: 741–761.

———. 2004. Branded political communication: Lifestyle politics, logo campaigns, and the rise of global citizenship. In *Politics, products, and markets*, eds. Michele Micheletti, Andreas Follesdal, and Dietlind Stolle, 101–126. New Brunswick, NJ: Transaction Publishers.

Berliner, Joseph S. 1957. *Factory and manager in the USSR.* Cambridge, MA: Harvard University Press.

Bernstein, Marver. 1955. *Regulating business by independent commission.* Princeton, NJ: Princeton University Press.

Berry, Jeffrey M. 1999. *The new liberalism: The rising power of citizen groups.* Washington, DC: The Brookings Institution.

Blais, Andre, Elizabeth Gidengil, Niel Nevitte, and Richard Nadeau. 2004. The evolving nature of non-voting: Evidence from Canada. *European Journal of Political Research* 43, no. 2: 221–223.

Bohstedt, John. 1998. Gender, household, and community politics: Women in English riots, 1790–1810. *Past and Present* 120: 88–122.

Boliek, Brooks. 2003. Dixie Chicks' radio ban on Senate panel hit list. *Hollywood Reporter.* July 9. www.hollywoodreporter.com/hr/search/article display.jsp?vnu content id'1930521 (accessed January 23, 2010).

Bosso, Christopher. 2005. *Environment, Inc.: From grassroots to beltway.* Lawrence: University Press of Kansas.

Bradsher, Keith. 2008. China offers plan to clean up its polluted lakes. *New York Times.* January 23. www.nytimes.com/2008/01/23/world/asia/23china.html (accessed January 23, 2010).

Burns, Nancy, Kay Schlozman, and Sidney Verba. 2001. *The private roots of public action: Gender, equality, and political participation.* Cambridge, MA: Harvard University Press.

Chase, Michael, and James Mulvenon. 2002. *You've got dissent! Chinese dissident use of the Internet and Beijing's counter-strategies.* Santa Monica, CA: RAND.

Clarke, Betty. 2003. The Dixie Chicks: Shepherd's Bush empire, London [performance review]. *Guardian.* March 12. www.guardian.co.uk.music/2003/mar/12/ artsfeatures.popandrock (accessed January 23, 2010).

CNN.com/Entertainment. 2003. Dixie Chicks pulled from air after bashing Bush. CNN.com. March 14. www.cnn.com/2003/SHOWBIZ/Music/03/14/dixie .chicks.reut (accessed January 23, 2010).

Corporate Social Responsibility Newswire. 2004. Global warming resolutions at U.S. oil companies bring policy commitments from leaders, and record high votes at

Laggards. Corporate Social Responsibility Newswire. May 13. www.csrwire.com/press/press_release/23395-Global-Warming-Resolutions-at-U-S-Oil-Companies-Bring-Policy-Commitments-from-Leaders-and-Record-High-Votes-at-Laggards (accessed December 21, 2009).

Cosgrove-Mather, Bootie. 2005. Group ends Disney boycott: Conservative Christian group had boycotted Disney for nine years. CBSNews.com. May 24. www.cbsnews.com/stories/2005/05/24/entertainment/main697567.shmtl (accessed January 23, 2010).

Dahl, Robert A. 1961. *Who governs?* New Haven, CT: Yale University Press.

Dalton, Russell J. 2008. Citizenship norms and the expansion of political participation. *Political Studies* 56: 76–98.

Dalton, Russell J., and Martin P. Wattenberg, eds. 2000. *Parties without partisans.* New York: Oxford University Press.

Danaher, Kevin, and Roger Burbach, eds. 2000. *Globalize this! The battle against the World Trade Organization and corporate rule.* Monroe, ME: Common Courage Press.

Della Porta, Donatella, ed. 2007. *The global justice movement: Cross-national and transnational perspectives.* Boulder, CO: Paradigm Publishers.

Democracy Now! 2007. Shut up and sing! Dixie Chicks' big Grammy win caps comeback from backlash over anti-war stance [audio and print]. Democracy Now! February 15. www.democracynow.org/2007/2/15/shut_up_and_sing_dixie_chicks (accessed January 23, 2010).

Dumke, Mick. 2007. Critical mass: Under mounting pressure from citizens, can Chicago come up with a recycling plan that actually works? *Chicago Reader* (October 25): 23, 25–28.

Edelman, Murray. 1964. *The symbolic uses of politics.* Urbana: University of Illinois Press.

Eliasoph, Nina. 1998. *Avoiding politics: How Americans produce apathy in everyday life.* Cambridge, UK: Cambridge University Press.

European Social Survey (ESS). 2009. ESS round 1—2002. ESS Data. http://ess.nsd.uib.no/ess/round1 (accessed January 23, 2010).

Feigenbaum, Harvey B., Jeffrey Henig, and Chris Hamnett. 1998. *Shrinking the state: Political underpinnings of privatization.* Cambridge, UK: Cambridge University Press.

Fiorina, Morris P. 2002. Parties, participation, and representation in America: Old theories face new realities. In *Political science: State of the discipline*, eds. Ira Katznelson and Helen Milner, 511–541. New York: Norton.

Fisher, Dana R., and William R. Freudenburg. 2001. Ecological modernization and its critics: Assessing the past and looking toward the future. *Society and Natural Resources* 14: 701–709.

Fishkin, James S. 1992. *The dialogue of justice: Toward a self-reflective society.* New Haven, CT: Yale University Press.

Foote, Donna. 2000. Erin fights Goliath. *Newsweek.* March 13. www.newsweek.com/id/83320 (accessed January 23, 2010).

Frey, Darcey. 2002. How green is BP? *New York Times Magazine*. December 8. www .mindfully.org/Industry/BP-How-Green8dec02.htm (accessed January 23, 2010).

Friedman, Milton, and Rose Friedman. 1980. *Free to choose: A personal statement.* New York: Harcourt Brace Jovanovich.

Friedman, Monroe. 1996. A positive approach to organized consumer action: The "buycott" as an alternative to the boycott. *Journal of Consumer Policy* 19, no. 4: 439–451.

———. 1999. *Consumer boycotts: Effecting change through the marketplace and the media.* New York: Routledge.

Galtung, Fredrik, and Jeremy Pope. 1999. The global coalition against corruption: Evaluating Transparency International. In *The self-restraining state: Power and accountability in new democracies*, eds. Andreas Schedler, Larry Diamond, and Marc F. Plattner, 257–282. Boulder, CO: Lynne Rienner Publishers.

Glickman, Lawrence B. 2005. "Making lisle the style": The politics of fashion in the Japanese silk boycott, 1937–1940. *Journal of Social History* 38, no. 3: 573–608.

Greenhouse, Steven. 1998. Anti-sweatshop coalition finds itself at odds on garment factory code. *New York Times.* July 3. www.nytimes.com/1998/07/03/us/anti-sweatshop-coalition-finds-itself-at-odds-on-garment-factory-code.html?emc=eta1 (accessed January 23, 2010).

Greenpeace. 2007. ExxonMobil's continued funding of global warming denial industry. ExxonSecrets. May. www.exxonsecrets.org and also www.greenpeace.org (accessed April 2008).

Griffiths, Catherine. 2009. Consumption as political participation: An exploratory look at political consumerism in four post-Communist countries. Working paper, Political Science Department, University of Illinois, Chicago.

Hadden, Jennifer, and Sidney Tarrow. 2007. The global justice movement in the United States since Seattle. In *The global justice movement: Cross-national and transnational perspectives*, ed. Donatella della Porta, 210–231. Boulder, CO: Paradigm Publishers.

Hardin, Garrett James, and John Baden. 1977. *The tragedy of the commons.* San Francisco: W. H. Freeman.

Harr, Jonathan. 1996. *A civil action.* New York: Vintage.

Hays, Samuel P. 1964. The politics of reform in municipal government in the Progressive Era. *Pacific Northwest Quarterly* 55: 157–169.

Heclo, Hugh. 1978. Issue networks and the executive establishment. In *The new American political system*, ed. Anthony King, 87–124. Washington, DC: American Enterprise Institute.

Heidenheimer, Arnold J., and Michael Johnston, eds. 2002. *Political corruption: Concepts and contexts.* New Brunswick, NJ: Transaction Publishers.

Hofstadter, Richard. 1955. *The age of reform: From Bryan to FDR.* New York: Vintage.

Holzer, Boris. 2007. Framing the corporation: Royal Dutch/Shell and human rights woes in Nigeria. *Journal of Consumer Policy* 30: 281–301.

Hooge, Marc, and Dietlind Stolle, eds. 2003. *Generating social capital: Civil society and institutions in comparative perspective*. New York: Palgrave Press.

Howard, Marc Morjé. 2002. The weakness of postcommunist civil society. *Journal of Democracy* 13, no. 1: 157–169.

Inglehart, Ronald. 1997. *Modernization and postmodernization: Cultural, economic and political change in 43 societies*. Princeton, NJ: Princeton University Press.

———. 2000. Globalization and postmodern values. *Washington Quarterly* 23, no. 1: 215–228.

Instituttet for Fremtidsforsning and Elsam. 1996. *Den politiske forbruger*. Copenhagen: Elsam.

Jenkins, J. Craig. 1985. *The politics of insurgency: The farm worker movement in the 1960s*. New York: Columbia University Press.

Jones, Bryan D., and Frank R. Baumgartner. 2005. *The politics of attention: How government prioritizes problems*. Chicago: University of Chicago Press.

Jones, Charles O. 1975. *Clean air: The policies and politics of pollution control*. Pittsburgh, PA: University of Pittsburgh Press.

Jordan, Grant. 2001. *Shell, Greenpeace and the Brent Spar*. Basingstoke, UK: Palgrave.

Kahn, Joseph. 2007. In China, a lake's champion imperils himself. *New York Times*. October 14. www.nytimes.com/2007/10/14/world/asia/14china.html (accessed January 23, 2010).

Karklins, Rasma. 2005. *The system made me do it: Corruption in post-Communist societies*. Armonk, NY: M. E. Sharpe.

Keck, Margaret E., and Kathryn Sikkink. 1998. *Activists beyond borders: Advocacy networks in international politics*. Ithaca, NY: Cornell University Press.

Klein, Naomi. 2000. *No logo*. Picador: New York.

Klotz, Audie. 1995. *Norms in international relations: The struggle against apartheid*. Ithaca, NY: Cornell University Press.

Krauss, Clifford, and Jad Mouawad. 2007. Exxon chief cautions against rapid action to cut carbon emissions. *New York Times*. February 14. www.nytimes.com/2007/02/14/business/14exxon.html (accessed January 23, 2010).

Kristof, Nicholas D. 2009. Tear down this cyberwall! *New York Times*. June 18. www.nytimes.com/2009/06/18opinion/18/kristof.html (accessed January 23, 2010).

Krugman, Paul. 2006. Enemy of the planet. *New York Times*. April 17. http://select.nytimes.com/2006/04/17/opinion/17krugman.html (accessed January 23, 2010).

Kuper, Andrew. 2004. *Democracy beyond borders: Justice and representation in global institutions*. New York: Oxford University Press.

Landler, Mark, and Brian Stetler. 2009. With a hint to Twitter, Washington taps into a potent new force in diplomacy. *New York Times*. June 18. www.nytimes.com/2009/06/29/business/media/29coverage.html (accessed January 23, 2010).

Lazic, Mladen. 1999. *Protest in Belgrade: Winter of discontent*. Budapest: Central European University Press.

Leeds, Jeff. 2006. How the Dixie Chicks hit the charts without radio support. *New*

York Times. June 10. www.nytimes.com/2006/06/10/arts/music/10chic.html (accessed January 23, 2010).

Leeds, Jeff, and Lorne Manly. 2007. Defiant Dixie Chicks are big winners at the Grammys. *New York Times.* February 12. www.nytimes.com/2007/02/12/arts/music/12gram.html (accessed January 23, 2010).

Levi, Margaret, and April Linton. 2003. Fair trade: A cup at a time? *Politics and Society* 31: 407–432.

Li, Lianjiang, and Kevin J. O'Brien. 1999. The struggle over village elections. In *The paradox of China's post-Mao reforms,* eds. Merle Goldman and Roderick MacFarquhar, 129–144. Cambridge, MA: Harvard University Press.

Link, Arthur S. 1954. *Woodrow Wilson and the Progressive Era, 1910–1917.* New York: Harper.

Lowi, Theodore J., Jr. 1979. *The end of liberalism.* Rev. ed. New York: W. W. Norton.

Macalister, Terry. 2003. Shell chief delivers global warming warning to Bush in his own back yard. *Guardian.* March 12. www.guardian.co.uk/environment/2003/mar/12/usnews.business (accessed January 23, 2010).

Mansbridge, Jane J. 1983. *Beyond adversarial democracy.* Chicago: University of Chicago Press.

Marquette, Heather. 2003. *Corruption, politics, and development: The role of the World Bank.* Basingstoke, UK: Palgrave Macmillan.

Mazmanian, Daniel, and Paul A. Sabatier. 1989. *Implementation and public policy.* Lanham, MD: University Press of America.

McAdam, Doug. 1999. *Political process and the development of black insurgency, 1930–1970.* Rev. ed. Chicago: University of Chicago Press.

McConnell, Grant. 1966. *Private power and American democracy.* New York: Knopf.

McFarland, Andrew S. 1976. *Public interest lobbies: Decision making on energy.* Washington, DC: American Enterprise Institute.

———. 1984. *Common cause: Lobbying in the public interest.* Chatham, NJ: Chatham House.

———. 1993. *Cooperative pluralism: The national coal policy experiment.* Lawrence: University Press of Kansas.

———. 2004. *Neopluralism: The evolution of political process theory.* Lawrence: University Press of Kansas.

McFaul, Michael. 2005. Transitions from postcommunism. *Journal of Democracy* 16: 5–19.

Melucci, Alberto. 1996. *Challenging codes: Collective action in the information age.* Cambridge, UK: Cambridge University Press.

Merton, Robert K. 1957. *Social theory and social structure.* Rev. ed. New York: Free Press.

Micheletti, Michele. 2001. Shopping as political participation: The role of women in political consumption. Paper presented at the annual meeting of the American

Political Science Association, August 29, in San Francisco, California. See page 65 of the APSA 2001 program.

———. 2003. *Political virtue and shopping: Individuals, consumerism, and collective action.* New York: Palgrave Macmillan.

———. 2004. Why more women? Issues of gender and political consumerism. In *Politics, products, and markets,* eds. Michele Micheletti, Andreas Follesdal, and Dietlind Stolle, 245–264. New Brunswick, NJ: Transaction Publishers.

Micheletti, Michele, and Andreas Follesdal. 2007. Shopping for human rights: An Introduction to the special issue. *Journal of Consumer Policy* 30: 167–175.

Micheletti, Michele, Andreas Follesdal, and Dietlind Stolle. 2004. *Politics, products, and markets: Exploring political consumerism past and present.* New Brunswick, NJ: Transaction Publishers.

Micheletti, Michele, and Andrew S. McFarland, eds. 2010. *Creative participation: Responsibility-taking in a political world.* Boulder, CO: Paradigm Publishers.

Mowry, George E. 1958. *The era of Theodore Roosevelt, 1900–1912.* New York: Hill & Wang.

Moynihan, Daniel Patrick. 1969. *Maximum feasible misunderstanding: Community action in the war on poverty.* New York: Free Press.

MSNBC. 2007. Exxon cuts ties to global warming skeptics. MSNBC. January 12. www .msnbc.com/id/16593606 (accessed January 23, 2010).

Muller, Mike. 1974. *The baby killer.* London: War on Want.

National Petroleum Council. 2007. Facing the hard truths about energy. Hard Truths. July. www.npchardtruthsreport.org (accessed January 23, 2010).

New York Times. 2005. Religion: Baptists end Disney boycott. *New York Times.* June 23. http://query.nytimes.com/gst/fullpage.html?res=9A03E4DE1F3BF930A157 55C0A9639C8B63 (accessed January 23, 2010).

Nocera, Joe. 2007. Exxon Mobil just wants to be loved. *New York Times.* February 10. www.nytimes.com/2007/02/10/business/10nocera.html (accessed January 23, 2010).

Norris, Pippa. 1999. *Critical citizens: Global support for democratic government.* New York: Oxford University Press.

———. 2002a. Democratic Phoenix: Agencies, repertoires, and targets of political activism. Paper presented at the annual meeting of the American Political Science Association, August 29 to September 1, in Boston, Massachusetts.

———. 2002b. *Democratic phoenix: Reinventing political activism.* Cambridge, UK: Cambridge University Press.

O'Brien, Kevin J., and Lianjiang Li. 2006. *Rightful resistance in rural China.* Cambridge, UK: Cambridge University Press.

Olson, Mancur, Jr. 1965. *The logic of collective action.* Cambridge, MA: Harvard University Press.

Orfield, Gary. 1975. *Congressional power: Congress and social change.* New York: Harcourt Brace Jovanovich.

Orleck, Annelise. 1993. "We are the mythical thing called the public": Militant housewives during the Great Depression. *Feminist Studies* 19: 147–172.

Orum, Anthony M. 2001. *Introduction to political sociology.* 4th ed. Upper Saddle River, NJ: Prentice Hall.

Ostrom, Elinor. 1990. *Governing the commons: The evolution of institutions for collective action.* Cambridge, UK: Cambridge University Press.

Pareles, Jon. 2006. The Dixie Chicks: America catches up with them. *New York Times.* May 21. www.nytimes.com/2006/05/21/arts/music/21pare.html (accessed January 23, 2010).

Pateman, Carole. 1970. *Participation and democratic theory.* Cambridge, UK: Cambridge University Press.

Pellizzoni, Luigi. 2007. Three challenges for political consumerism. Paper presented at the Nordic Consumer Policy Research Conference, October 3–5, in Helsinki, Finland.

Pianta, Mario, and Raffaele Marchetti. 2007. The global justice movements: The transnational dimension. In *The global justice movement: Cross-national and transnational perspectives,* ed. Donatella della Porta, 29–51. Boulder, CO: Paradigm Publishers.

Pitkin, Hanna Fenichel. 1967. *The concept of representation.* Berkeley: University of California Press.

Piven, Frances Fox, and Richard A. Cloward. 1977. *Poor people's movements.* New York: Pantheon Books.

Pressman, Jeffrey L., and Aaron Wildavsky. 1973. *Implementation.* Berkeley: University of California Press.

Putnam, Robert D. 1995. Bowling alone: America's declining social capital. *Journal of Democracy* 6, no. 1: 65–78.

———. 2000. *Bowling alone: The collapse and revival of American community.* New York: Simon & Schuster.

Riordan, William L. 1963. *Plunkitt of Tammany Hall.* New York: Knopf.

Ripley, Randall B., and Grace A. Franklin. 1984. *Congress, the bureaucracy, and public policy.* 3rd ed. Homewood, IL: Dorsey Press.

Rose-Ackerman, Susan. 1999. *Corruption and government: Causes, consequences, and reform.* Cambridge, UK: Cambridge University Press.

Rossman, Gabriel. 2004. Elites, masses, and media blacklists: The Dixie Chicks controversy. *Social Forces* 83, no. 1: 61–79.

Rothenberg, Lawrence S. 1992. *Linking citizens to government: Interest group politics at common cause.* Cambridge, UK: Cambridge University Press.

Rousseau, Jean-Jacques. 1984 [1754]. *Discourse on the origin of inequality.* Part II. Ed. and trans. Maurice Cranston. Harmondsworth, UK: Penguin Books.

Rucht, Dieter, Simon Teune, and Mundo Yang. 2007. The global justice movement in Great Britain. In *The global justice movement: Cross-national and transnational perspectives,* ed. Donatella della Porta, 128–156. Boulder, CO: Paradigm Publishers.

Russell, Clifford S., Signe Krarup, and Christopher Clark. 2005. Environment, information, and consumer behaviour: An introduction. In *Environment, information, and consumer behaviour*, eds. Signe Krarup and Clifford S. Russell, 1–29. Cheltenham, UK: Edward Elgar.

Sabatier, Paul A., and Hank C. Jenkins-Smith, eds. 1993. *Policy change and learning: An advocacy coalition approach.* Boulder, CO: Westview Press.

Saporito, Bill, with Tim Larimer, Bien Hoa, and Terry McCarthy. 1998. Taking a look inside Nike's factories. *Time.* March 30. www.time.com/time/magazine/article/0,9171,988059,00.html (accessed January 23, 2010).

Schattschneider, E. E. 1960. *The semisovereign people.* New York: Holt, Rinehart and Winston.

Sengupta, Somini. 2008. India grapples with how to convert its farmland into factories. *New York Times.* September 17. www.nytimes.com/2008/09/17/world/asia/17india.html (accessed January 10, 2010).

Sethi, S. Prakash. 1994. *Multinational corporations and the impact of public policy advocacy on corporate strategy: Nestle and the infant formula controversy.* Boston: Kluwer Academic Publishers.

Shaiko, Ronald G. 1999. *Voices and echoes for the environment: Public interest representation in the 1990s and beyond.* New York: Columbia University Press.

Skocpol, Theda. 2004. Voice and inequality: The transformation of American civic democracy. *Perspectives on Politics* 2: 3–20.

Smith, Jackie, et al. 2008. *Global democracy and the world social forums.* Boulder, CO: Paradigm Publishers.

Stolle, Dietlind, and Michele Micheletti. 2003. The gender gap reversed: Political consumerism as a women-friendly form of civic and political engagement: An exploratory study in Canada, Belgium and Sweden. Paper prepared for the Gender and Social Capital Conference, May 2–3, in Winnipeg, Canada.

Stolle, Dietlind, Marc Hooghe, and Michele Micheletti. 2005. Politics in the supermarket: Political consumption as a form of political participation. *International Political Science Review* 26, no. 245: 245–269.

Svendsen, Steen. 1995. Den politiske forbruger. *Fremtidsorientering* 4: 32–35. As referenced in Kristen Stromsnes, Political consumerism: A new kind of civic engagement? Paper presented at the CINEFOGO conference "Europe—With or Without You?" April 2, 2008, in Vienna, Austria.

Tarrow, Sidney. 2000. Mad cows and social activists: Contentious politics in the trilateral democracies. In *Disaffected democracies*, eds. Susan Pharr and Robert Putnam, 270–290. Princeton, NJ: Princeton University Press.

Thelen, David P. 1972. *The new citizenship: Origins of progressivism in Wisconsin, 1885–1900.* Columbia: University of Missouri Press.

Tran, Mark. 2005. Branded. *Guardian.* September 1. http://blogs.guardian.co.uk/businessinsight/archives/2005/09/01/branded.html (accessed January 23, 2010).

Transparency International. 2008. *Transparency International's annual report 2007.* Transparency International. June. www.transparency.org/publications/annual_report (accessed January 23, 2010).

Tucker, Joshua A. 2007. Enough! Electoral fraud, collective action problems, and post-Communist colored revolutions. *Perspectives on Politics* 5: 535–552.

Tyrangiel, Josh. 2006. Chicks in the line of fire. *Time.* May 21. www.time.com/time/magazine/article/0,9171,1196419,00.html (accessed January 23, 2010).

Unger, Nancy C. 2000. *Fighting Bob La Follette: The righteous reformer.* Chapel Hill: University of North Carolina Press.

Van Deth, Jan W. 2008. "Is creative participation creative democracy?" Working paper, Mannheim Center for European Social Research, Mannheim University (Germany), September 19, typescript.

———. 2010. Is creative participation creative democracy? In *Creative participation: Responsibility-taking in a political world,* eds. Michele Micheletti and Andrew S. McFarland. Boulder, CO: Paradigm Publishers.

Vanhuysse, Pieter. 2004. East European protest politics in the early 1990s: Comparative trends and preliminary theories. *Europe-Asia Studies* 56, no. 3: 421–438.

Verba, Sidney, and Norman Nie. 1972. *Participation in America: Political democracy and social equality.* New York: Harper & Row.

Verba, Sidney, Kay Lehman Schlozman, and Henry E. Brady. 1995. *Voice and equality: Civic voluntarism in American politics.* Cambridge, MA: Harvard University Press.

Vogel, David. 1989. *Fluctuating fortunes: The political power of business in America.* New York: Basic Books.

———. 2005. *The market for virtue: The potential and limits of corporate social responsibility.* Washington, DC: Brookings Institution.

Walker, Jack L., Jr. 1991. *Mobilizing interest groups in America.* Ann Arbor: University of Michigan Press.

Wattenberg, Martin P. 2002. *Where have all the voters gone?* Cambridge, MA: Harvard University Press.

Weidenbaum, Murray. 1979. *The future of business regulation: Private action and public demand.* New York: AMACOM.

Weinstein, James. 1968. *The corporate ideal and the liberal state, 1900–1918.* Boston: Beacon.

Wiebe, Robert H. 1967. *The search for order, 1877–1920.* New York: Hill and Wang.

Wikipedia. Dixie Chicks. Wikipedia. http://en.wikipedia.org/wiki/Dixie_Chicks (accessed April 2, 2009).

Wilcox, Clyde. 1992. *God's warriors: The Christian Right in twentieth-century America.* Baltimore: Johns Hopkins Press.

Wilkinson, John. 2007. Fair trade: Dynamics and dilemmas of a market oriented global social movement. *Journal of Consumer Policy* 30: 219–239.

Williams, Melissa. 1998. *Voice, trust, and memory: Marginalized groups and the failings of liberal representation.* Princeton, NJ: Princeton University Press.

Woburn Hydrogeology Data. Brief history. Woburn Hydrogeology Data. www.et.byu.edu/groups/ce547/woburn/briefhistory.php (accessed March 30, 2009).

Young, Iris Marion. 2006. Responsibility and global justice: A social connection model. *Social Philosophy and Policy* 23: 102–130.

Index

❧
About the Author

Andrew S. McFarland is professor of political science and a fellow of the Institute for the Humanities at the University of Illinois at Chicago. He has published three books about creative participation as public interest lobbying in America, including *Public Interest Lobbies: Decision Making on Energy* (Washington, DC: American Enterprise Institute for Public Policy Research, 1976), *Common Cause: Lobbying in the Public Interest* (Chatham, NJ: Chatham House Publishers, 1984), and *Cooperative Pluralism: The National Coal Policy Experiment* (Lawrence: University Press of Kansas, 1994). His most recent book on this theme is *Creative Participation: Responsibility-Taking in the Political World,* coedited with Michele Micheletti (Boulder, CO: Paradigm Publishers, 2010). He has coedited *Social Movements and American Political Institutions* with Anne N. Costain (Lanham, MD: Rowman & Littlefield, 1998) and published *Neopluralism: The Evolution of Political Process Theory* (Lawrence: University Press of Kansas, 2004).